The Mysterious & Unknown

Sorcery

Other titles in *The Mysterious & Unknown* series:

The Bermuda Triangle
Crop Circles
The Loch Ness Monster
Mummies
Paranormal Activity
Prophecies and Soothsayers
Pyramids
Urban Legends
Vampires
Werewolves

The Mysterious & Unknown

Sorcery

by Stuart A. Kallen

ReferencePoint Press®

San Diego, CA

©2012 ReferencePoint Press, Inc.
Printed in the United States

For more information, contact:
ReferencePoint Press, Inc.
PO Box 27779
San Diego, CA 92198
www.ReferencePointPress.com

LIBRARY OF CONGRESS CATALOGING-IN-PUBLICATION DATA

Kallen, Stuart A., 1955–
   Sorcery / by Stuart A. Kallen.
      p. cm. — (The mysterious & unknown)
   Includes bibliographical references and index.
   ISBN-13: 978-1-60152-242-9 (hardback)
   ISBN-10: 1-60152-242-8 (hardback)
1. Occultism. 2. Magic. 3. Witchcraft. I. Title.
   BF1411.K35   2012
   133.4—dc23
                                                    2011038861

CONTENTS

FOREWORD

"Strange is our situation here upon earth."
—*Albert Einstein*

Since the beginning of recorded history, people have been perplexed, fascinated, and even terrified by events that defy explanation. While science has demystified many of these events, such as volcanic eruptions and lunar eclipses, some remain outside the scope of the provable. Do UFOs exist? Are people abducted by aliens? Can some people see into the future? These questions and many more continue to puzzle, intrigue, and confound despite the enormous advances of modern science and technology.

It is these questions, phenomena, and oddities that Reference-Point Press's *The Mysterious & Unknown* series is committed to exploring. Each volume examines historical and anecdotal evidence as well as the most recent theories surrounding the topic in debate. Fascinating primary source quotes from scientists, experts, and eyewitnesses as well as in-depth sidebars further inform the text. Full-color illustrations and photos add to each book's visual appeal. Finally, source notes, a bibliography, and a thorough index provide further reference and research support. Whether for research or the curious reader, *The Mysterious & Unknown* series is certain to satisfy those fascinated by the unexplained.

INTRODUCTION

Making Magic

In 1580 the prominent French lawyer Jean Bodin wrote, "A sorcerer is one who, by commerce with the Devil, has a full intention of attaining his own ends."[1] In Bodin's time, sorcery was a symbol of all evil, associated with sinister spirits and supernatural monsters. Sorcerers were practitioners of magic but they also possessed knowledge of herbs, plants, gems and minerals, and of the stars and planets. In a time of widespread ignorance and illiteracy, wisdom gleaned from ancient religious texts and obscure magic books contributed to the mysteries of the sorcerer's magic. Sorcerers, it was thought, could harness the forces of nature, create powerful mind-bending potions and powders, predict the future, and control the actions of those who sought their advice, as well as those who did not.

Sorcerers found recipes for magic in spell books called grimoires. The term *grimoire* is derived from the French word for "grammar"—*grammaire*. Grammar is a set of rules and principles for how words and their component parts combine to form proper sentences. A grimoire is a set of magical words with instructions on how to combine them for successful spells.

At various times and in various places, those known as wizards, witches, warlocks, magicians, and enchanters were called sorcerers and accused of practicing sorcery. Though sorcerers were sometimes revered for their wisdom and knowledge, they were more often feared and persecuted. Between 1450 and 1750 about 100,000 women and men were tortured and executed for practicing sorcery in Europe. Some were killed by hysterical mobs, others by government or church officials after lengthy trials.

Good Versus Evil

For centuries, a legendary wizard named Merlin was by far the most famous sorcerer in the world. Merlin first appeared in a history of British kings written around 1136 AD by a cleric known as Geoffrey of Monmouth. In the centuries that followed, Merlin's magical powers became the stuff of legend. Among them were his ability to shape-shift, appearing at various times as a stag, a wise old man, a fresh-faced teen, and a giant herdsman, who was 18 feet (5.4m) tall with a head as large as a buffalo and a beard down to the ground.

Today the most famous sorcerer is undoubtedly Harry Potter, the fictional wizard in the best-selling series of fantasy novels by British author J.K. Rowling. Like sorcerers from ancient times, Potter and his fellow wizards and witches use magic spells, rituals, and charms to change the outcome of events. Potter uses his magic for good, battling dark powers and evil sorcerers.

As in the Harry Potter books, the conflict between good and evil has long been a characteristic of sorcery. In ancient tribal societies, sorcery was seen as necessary for survival. People believed magic rituals could be used to peel back the thin tissue that separated physical reality and the spiritual world. By stepping into the supernatural dimension, sorcerers walked with spirits.

They could control forces that ruled nature and speak with the gods and goddesses that ruled the universe. Such pursuits allowed sorcerers to cure the sick and insure success during hunts

Wizards, witches, and magicians have all been accused of sorcery at one time or another. Relying on their knowledge of plants, stars, and rocks for the practice of magic, they conveyed to the illiterate and ignorant masses a sense that they possessed special powers.

The shamanistic
practices of
sorcerers date
back at least
20,000 years
and have been
observed among
the indigenous
people of Africa,
Asia, Australia, and
the Americas.

and battles. Sorcerers could also conduct rituals to bring love to the lovelorn, inflict pain on the wicked, and kill enemies in horrible, unnatural ways.

The melding of good and bad associated with sorcery can even be seen in the origins of the word *wizard*. The term is derived from the Old English term *wys*, for "wise," because sorcerers were originally known for their wisdom. However, 1,000 years ago wizards were feared for their single-minded dedication to magic. According to British occult expert P.G. Maxwell-Stuart, the *ard* sound in *wizard* indicated "someone who does something [like practicing sorcery] to excess, or who does something that is discreditable . . . therefore 'wizard' sounds a negative, critical note."[2]

Drumming Shamans

The ways of the wizard have been kept alive by sorcerers, or shamans, who live in the frozen forests of Siberia, in northeastern Russia. These shamans are respected members of the indigenous Tungas tribe. Drawing on ceremonies that date back thousands of years, they communicate with the spirits of plants and animals and perform healing rituals for the sick and injured. During bizarre rituals that involve drumming, dancing, and mind-bending hallucinogenic mushrooms, shamans purportedly locate game, peer into the future, and control the weather. Some also practice black magic.

The shamanistic practices of sorcerers date back at least 20,000 years and have been observed among the indigenous people of Africa, Asia, Australia, and the Americas. Sorcery is still practiced in modern times by voodoo priests in Haiti, by shamans in Peru and Mexico, and by wizards in Africa. Self-proclaimed sorcerers and shamans can also be found in Europe and the United States.

The Music of the Universe

During the past 100 years, science and technology have transformed the planet. Electricity, cars, airplanes, televisions, computers, and advanced medicine are taken for granted in modern times. But these wonders would have been seen as magic in earlier centuries.

Despite widespread faith in modern technology, some continue to believe that the world can be manipulated by magic. As Maxwell-Stuart writes, there is a "child-like desire for wonders and instant gratification which magic may be called on to satisfy."[3] Those desires drive people to light candles, burn incense, mix herbal potions, chant spells, and dance beneath the moonlit sky in hopes of manipulating the supernatural world. And the sorcerer who achieves that state of heightened perception has no need for a cell phone or MP3 player. He or she is communicating with the spirits and hearing the music of the universe.

Nonbelievers may dismiss such claims. Skeptics say sorcery does not exist and sorcerers are deluded. But the mysteries that lurk beyond the senses are little understood and remain invisible to most. In the world of the unknown, sorcery is power, and people are hungry for power no matter what the time or place.

CHAPTER 1

Sorcery Through the Ages

In 1530 the renowned Italian painter and author Benvenuto Cellini struck up a conversation with a man who said he was a sorcerer. The man invited Cellini to join him in a magical ritual. Cellini agreed and brought his 12-year-old shop assistant with him to witness the event. Cellini met the sorcerer at the famed Colosseum in Rome late at night, when the arena was deserted. The sorcerer traced circles on the ground and set fire to some coal. He handed Cellini a charm decorated with a pentacle and other magical symbols and instructed him to stand within one of the circles. Handfuls of incense and herbs were thrown upon the coal. The sorcerer spoke words read from a grimoire. In his book *Autobiography of Benvenuto Cellini*, Cellini describes what happened next:

> [The sorcerer] began to utter those awful invocations, calling by name on multitudes of demons

who are captains of their legions, and these he summoned by the virtue and potency of God, the Uncreated, Living, and Eternal, in phrases of the Hebrew, and also of the Greek and Latin tongues; insomuch that in a short space of time the whole Colosseum was full of a hundredfold [spirits]. . . . [My young assistant] shrieked out in terror that a million of the fiercest men were swarming round and threatening us. He said, moreover, that four huge giants had appeared, who were striving to force their way inside the circle. Meanwhile the [sorcerer], trembling with fear, kept doing his best with mild and soft persuasions to dismiss them.[4]

Cellini wrote his book during the Renaissance, a period between 1350 and the early 1500s when there was an intense interest in classical Greek art and literature. During the Renaissance, scholars were translating ancient grimoires from classical Greek into Latin, French, Italian, and English. The books, written around 300 BC, were being used by Renaissance sorcerers to call up spirits, angels, and demons. In Cellini's case it seems the sorcerer was not powerful enough to control the mystical powers his magical words had unleashed.

The *Greek Magical Papyri*

While Cellini does not mention the grimoire used in the spell, it is likely the sorcerer was reading from the ancient book *Papyri Graecae Magicae* (*Greek Magical Papyri*). The volume is a compilation of materials written between the second century BC and the fifth century AD. The text contains details of the complex tasks required of a sorcerer who is performing magical spells.

The Sword

In the following example of a spell called the Sword, from the grimoire *Papyri Graecae Magicae* (*Greek Magical Papyri*), the soul of any person can be immediately controlled by the sorcerer. The names of many powerful Greek deities and mythological characters associated with love, such as Aphrodite, Psyche, and Eros, are invoked. The magical terms, which are typical in ancient spells, appear to be unpronounceable gibberish but were purportedly understood by sorcerers and the gods:

> Take a magnetic stone . . . and engrave [the goddess] Aphrodite sitting astride Psyche and with her left hand holding on her hair bound in curls. And above her head: "ACHMAGE RARPEPSEI"; and below Aphrodite and Psyche engrave Eros standing on the vault of heaven, holding a blazing torch and burning Psyche. And below Eros these names: "ACHAPA ADONAIE BASMA CHARAKO IAKOB IAO E PHARPHAREI." On the other side of the stone engrave Psyche and Eros embracing one another and beneath Eros's feet these letters: "SSSSSSS," and beneath Psyche's feet: "EEEEEEE." Use the stone, when it has been engraved and consecrated, like this: put it under your tongue and turn it to what you wish and say [a] spell.

Papyri Graecae Magicae. Hermitic Library, 2011. http://hermetic.com.

These methods have appeared in countless grimoires since the Renaissance and have even been used for sorcery in the twenty-first century.

According to instructions in the *Greek Magical Papyri*, sorcerers must purify themselves before any ceremony can begin. This is done by avoiding certain foods, such as fish, considered polluting to the body. When it is time to conduct the ritual, the sorcerer must gather a wide range of materials, including a special lantern called a magician's lamp. This is filled with scented oil made with a mixture of rose petals and herbs such as spikenard. The sorcerer must build his own altar from wood or clay and obtain a chair with a high back for use as a spirit throne. Other sorcery items include a long ebony staff, a magical wand, flour, a jar of rainwater, various spices, wine, honey, small cakes, and milk.

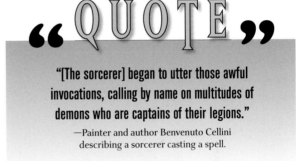

The *Greek Magical Papyri* recommends the sorcerer wait until sundown before carrying his magic instruments to a high hill or flat rooftop. A special robe must be worn, one that is made for the specific purpose of conducting magic rituals. After drawing a circle on the ground with charcoal, the sorcerer places a cake on the altar with other foods, such as honey and milk. Herbs and frankincense are placed on a burning coal, and the magic lamp is lit. With wand in hand, the sorcerer recites magical words from the grimoire such as "OROBASTRIA NEBOUTOSOUALETH."[5] These barely pronounceable words are followed by low-register utterances known today as overtone singing. In this process the sorcerer calls out magical

The Italian Renaissance artist and author Benvenuto Cellini (pictured) wrote of an encounter with a sorcerer who summoned dozens of demons— and barely managed to keep them from attacking Cellini and his assistant.

words, using breath control to create guttural sounds from the vocal chords. This type of singing has been employed by Tibetan monks for thousands of years. It is meant to transport the mind to the spiritual or supernatural world.

Magical words might also be written on small pieces of paper or the leaves of a laurel plant. These are burned in the magician's lamp. The names of various gods are invoked before the sorcerer calls up a daimon. While this term translates as "demon," it might refer to an evil spirit or a good angel, either of which would carry out the sorcerer's wishes.

As explained in *Greek Magical Papyri*, a hawk will announce the arrival of the daimon. The bird will fly directly to the sorcerer, stop in front of his face, and slap its wings together. According to the *Greek Magical Papyri*, when the spirit appears:

> A fiery star, coming down, will stand in the middle of the roof and . . . you will perceive the angel whom you besought, sent to you, and you will promptly learn the counsels of the gods. But don't you be afraid. Go up to the [angel], take his right hand, kiss him, and say these [magic spells] to the angel. For he will respond concisely to whatever you wish [to ask]. You, then, make him swear with this oath that he will remain inseparable from you and . . . will not disobey you at all.[6]

After the spirit takes a seat on the throne, more herbs are burned. The sorcerer expresses his desires to the spirit, perhaps inquiring about future events or methods to obtain riches. The spirit is then dismissed with a final chant or prayer.

Killing and Destroying

The *Greek Magical Papyri* covers a variety of sorcerer's rituals. Magicians may perform a binding ritual to attract and fasten a lover's will to him. Another spell restrains charioteers, presum-

Did You Know?

Sorcerers may perform a binding ritual to attract and bind a lover.

ably to keep soldiers in chariots from attacking. Other restraining spells involve repelling sickness, demons, and enemies. There are self-improvement spells to increase strength, memory, and mental powers. Perhaps the most useful spell describes a way to attract a supernatural assistant. According to the grimoire, this spirit provides many essential magical services:

> [He] sends dreams, he brings women, men . . . he kills, he destroys, he stirs up winds from the earth, he carries gold, silver, bronze, and he gives them to you whenever the need arises. And he frees from bonds a person chained in prison, he opens doors, he causes invisibility so that no one can see you at all, he is a bringer of fire, he brings water, wine, bread and [whatever] you wish in the way of foods: olive oil, vinegar.[7]

The aspects of killing and destroying were of great use to ancient sorcerers, who often seemed to be driven by revenge and hatred. The Greeks were notorious for this type of sorcery, known as curse magic. As the philosopher Plato wrote in *The Republic* in 360 BC, sorcerers "promise to harm an enemy, whether just or unjust, at a small cost; with magic arts and incantations binding [the gods], as they say, to execute their will."[8]

One of the most common tools used for the purpose of bringing harm was the curse tablet. The tablets were common in Greece, and their use was adopted by the Romans in later centuries. The tablet might be made from stone or wood, but tablets made from thin sheets of lead were preferable because the material is heavy, cold, and a sinister grey color. The instructions for the curse were carefully etched into the tablet with a sharp engraving tool called a stylus. The black magic verses included appeals to various gods to lend their supernatural powers to the curse. An example of a curse tablet was found near the British village of Uley in Gloucestershire in 1996. It was written in 150 BC, when the Romans ruled Britain. The sorcerer, named Honoratus, evokes the Roman god of commerce to harm a troublesome thief:

> Honoratus to the holy god Mercury. I complain to your divinity that I have lost two wheels and four cows and many small belongings from my house. I would ask . . . that you do not allow health to the person who has done me wrong, nor allow him to lie or sit or drink or eat, whether he is man or woman, whether boy or girl, whether slave or free, unless he brings my property to me. . . . [Make] me vindicated by your majesty.[9]

"Spellbound by Curse Tablets"

Other information on curse tablets might include magical words without obvious meaning. These consisted of a series of repeated vowels, symbols, or numbers representing letters. Sometimes called magical gibberish, these words might have been used by sorcerers simply to lend an air of mystery to the tablets. However, during past centuries, when most people were illiterate, the written word had immense power and was thought to be understood by the spirits and gods.

Once the tablet was created, the sorcerer folded or rolled the thin sheet of lead over the words so only the gods could read it. Tablets were pierced with several nails or pins. This helped bind or fix the curse to the victim. Some sorcerers were accused of using nails from crucifixions, a common form of punishment at the time. In the final step, the curse tablet was deposited in a shrine built to honor a specific deity. In the case of Honoratus, the tablet would be left at a shrine to Mercury.

Tablets might also be left where only the gods would find them, such as in a secluded forest. Some grimoires called for the curse tablet to be buried with the remains of an animal sacrificed for the spell. If the victim of the curse were known, the sorcerer might try to obtain a personal item, such as a lock of hair or piece of clothing, to be included in the burial.

Over 1,600 curse tablets have been unearthed by archeologists. The oldest, found in Sicily, dates to the late sixth century BC. More recent British examples were created up to the eighth century AD. Whenever they were created, curse tablets were widely feared. In the first century AD, the historian Pliny the Elder wrote, "There is no one who does not fear to be spellbound by curse tablets."[10]

"A Pact with the Devil"

Roman emperors feared sorcerers because they worried that magic might be used to threaten their power. When Christianity came to Rome in the fourth century AD, stern antisorcery laws were passed. Convicted sorcerers were either crucified or thrown to hungry lions before cheering crowds in the Colosseum. Laws also banned the simple possession of a grimoire, even by a high-ranking official. Personal libraries were searched for magic books, which were confiscated and publicly burned in the streets. The grimoire owner might have his property confiscated, face exile, or even be executed.

Roman laws published in AD 438 prohibited anyone from consulting with soothsayers, astrologers, enchanters, and various fortune-tellers called diviners, augurs, and seers. The term *maleficium*, which commonly referred to criminal acts such as theft and murder, was now used to describe sorcery. This word was later applied to all types of witches, sorcerers, and occultists, or those who believed in supernatural phenomena, until the end of the eighteenth century.

During the Middle Ages, between about 1,000 and 1,500 AD, theologians relentlessly equated sorcery with anti-Christian forces that were the enemy of all humanity. Sorcerers were accused of working in league with Satan and his demons, as medieval historians L.S. Davidson and J.O. Ward write:

> [By] the beginning of the fourteenth century in France, the view of *maleficium* as a criminal activity undertaken by an individual (sorcerer) using occult means for private advantage seems to have given way to a view of it as the practice of a sect of devil-worshippers, enemies of the larger community, who drew their occult power from a pact with the devil rather than from the correct performance of magical ritual. . . . [This] led the authorities to see themselves as defending Christendom against a satanic conspiracy.[11]

The First Sorcery Trial

The fear of sorcery reached the highest levels of power. In 1318 several members of the court of Pope John XXII were prosecuted for sorcery in Avignon, France. The action was likely political—the accused were seen as threats to the pope's power and were quickly executed. An English bishop named Richard Ledrede was present at the trials. Ledrede had been appointed bishop of the diocese of Ossory, near Kilkenny, Ireland, the previous year.

Watching the sorcery trials of high-placed papal officials, Ledrede came to understand that charges of sorcery could be very useful for someone wishing to gain power and wealth. In 1324 he decided to imitate the practices of the pope in his own diocese. In doing so, Ledrede initiated the first sorcery trial in Europe, in which the defendant, Lady Alice Kyteler, was accused of consorting with a sect of like-minded magicians who committed heinous crimes.

While innocent of the charges against her, Kyteler had a blemished past. In 1302, when she was about 22 years old, Kyteler's wealthy first husband, William Outlaw, died under mysterious circumstances. Kyteler was suspected of murdering Outlaw, aided by the man who became her second husband. Despite suspicions Kyteler was never put on trial for the crime. She went on to outlive the second husband—and a third husband—and inherited both of their fortunes. Around 1316 she married her fourth husband, Sir John le Poer, who was near death.

With great wealth, numerous marriages, and dozens of children and stepchildren, Kyteler's life resembled a modern-day soap opera. She had many enemies, including the more than 50 members of her extended family who sued one another in a variety of disputes, hoping to gain control of the family fortune.

Murder, Stupidity, and Affliction

In 1324 several of Kyteler's stepchildren accused her of using black magic. The charges were spelled out in great detail in docu-

Fear of sorcery reached the highest levels of power in 1318, when several high-ranking officials of the court of Pope John XXII (seated on throne) were executed on charges of sorcery. Many similar trials followed in later years.

ments that have been preserved for nearly 800 years. According to the stepchildren:

> [Kyteler used sorcery] to murder some of their fa-

thers and to infatuate others, reducing their senses to such stupidity that they gave all their possessions to her. . . . Moreover, the lady's present husband, the knight Sir John le Poer, had reached such a state through [magical] powders and lotions . . . that his whole body was emaciated, his nails were torn out and all his hair removed from his body.[12]

Ledrede himself had a number of financial disputes with Kyteler and hoped to use the charges of sorcery to siphon some of the family fortunes into the church coffers. When le Poer finally died, the bishop arrested Kyteler's maidservant, Petronilla of Meath. Ledrede whipped the woman before extracting a long, detailed confession. Petronilla said that, under orders from Kyteler, she had rejected Christ and made animal sacrifices to a demon named Robin Artisson, who hailed from the depths of the underworld. According to the charges, Petronilla admitted to making disgusting concoctions for the purposes of sorcery:

> [In] a skull from the head of a decapitated robber over a fire of oak wood, they would boil up the intestines and internal organs of [roosters] which . . . had been sacrificed to demons. They would mix in some horrible worms, add various herbs and countless other vile ingredients such as nails cut from dead bodies, hairs from the buttocks, and frequently also clothes from boys who had died before being baptized.[13]

These mixtures were used to make ointments that the sorcerer rubbed on the body while casting spells. Court documents charged that Kyteler chanted words that "would incite people to love and hate, to kill as well as afflict the bodies of faithful Christians, and do countless other things."[14]

Calling Up an Incubus

After providing the confession, Petronilla was charged with heresy. She became the first person burned at the stake for this crime in Ireland. In the following weeks, Kyteler and 11 family members were charged with seven serious crimes. These included denying faith in Christ, asking advice from demons, and having intimate relations with a male demon, or incubus. The incubus appeared at times as a shaggy black dog and on other occasions as an Ethiopian who carried an iron rod.

When the charges were filed, Kyteler and several of her children left Ireland. They likely fled to England, where they disappeared from the public record. Kyteler's oldest son, also named William Outlaw, tried to defend his mother in court. As a result, he was charged with numerous crimes, including heresy, perjury, and adultery, but received a relatively light sentence. He was ordered to spend a large sum of money to cover the cathedral roof with lead shingles. Ironically, the weight of the shingles caused the roof to collapse in a storm in 1332.

Others charged with sorcery in the Kyteler incident paid large debts of penance to the church as reparations for their sins. Ledrede thereby obtained the money he sought. However, the bishop's actions were seen as controversial, and church leaders and nobles forced him to flee Ireland. Soon after the trial, he took up residency in France. During the centuries that followed, church officials throughout Europe destroyed the lives of countless people by accusing them of sorcery. The last accused sorcerer was executed in Exeter, England, in 1684.

Magical Experiences

Attacks on witchcraft and sorcery in Europe drove its practitioners to conduct their affairs in secret. However, in the eighteenth century, a Swedish scientist and religious scholar named Emanuel Swedenborg led a magical revival based on his mystical visions.

Swedenborg was in his mid-50s in 1744 when he began having supernatural dreams. He claimed these spiritual experiences allowed him to visit heaven and hell, the moon, and various planets, including Jupiter, Mars, Venus, and Saturn. During these magical experiences, Swedenborg said he spoke with angels, demons, and spirits of the dead. Swedenborg, who claimed to be guided by God, also claimed to have psychic powers that allowed him to see into the future or envision events taking place hundreds of miles away.

Swedenborg wrote numerous books about his experiences, and the texts formed the basis of a religious movement called Swedenborgianism, or the New Church. While Swedenborg never revealed the methods he used to visit outer space or converse with spirits, he is credited with reviving interest in spiritualism, the occult, and sorcery. By the mid-nineteenth century, his books inspired an unprecedented magical revival in Europe and the United States.

Ongoing Practice and Beliefs

Sorcery became stylish in the nineteenth century, when many well-known authors, actors, and even politicians defied traditional religious conventions to take an active interest in magic. In England during the 1880s, members of the Hermetic Order of the Golden Dawn openly proclaimed themselves to be sorcerers. In the United States the spiritualist Helena Blavatsky became a celebrity for her alleged powers to speak to the dead and to predict the future. Interest in sorcery continues today among New Age believers, who call themselves shamans, wizards, sorcerers, witches, and Wiccans. These people practice ancient sorcery techniques involving trances, divination, and healing the sick with herbs or crystals.

Modern sorcerers tend to ignore negative aspects traditionally associated with the practice, such as black magic, demons, and curses. Instead, the New Age magicians focus on spells that bring mental and physical health or attract love, money, and spiritual harmony.

Whether they call themselves Wiccans or wizards, countless people consider themselves sorcerers in the twenty-first century. Some live in the suburbs; others are shamans who reside deep in the Amazon rain forest. Wherever they are, the self-proclaimed sorcerers practice traditions that date back to the dawn of history. Whether a person can find love or money by lighting a candle and chanting some magical words remains a matter of debate. That has not stopped people from trying to do so in the past, and it certainly will not stop them in the future.

CHAPTER 2

Sorcerers and Ceremonies

The work of sorcerers down through the ages has long been based on conducting magical rituals or ceremonies. When conducting ceremonial magic, sometimes referred to as high magic, the sorcerer follows instructions from a grimoire. He or she wears specific clothing, recites precise spells, and uses a variety of potions and powders meant to attract spirits and facilitate magic.

Records of long, complex, and elaborate magic ceremonies date back thousands of years to ancient Egypt, Greece, and Rome. However, beginning in the middle of the nineteenth century, these methods of sorcery were revised and rewritten by a few dedicated European sorcerers.

The revival of modern ceremonial sorcery began when a French magician and occult author named Eliphas Levi traveled to England to study with scholars of philosophy. In 1854 Levi published *The Dogma of the High Magic*, which was translated into

English in 1896 by Arthur E. Waite, a scholar of mysticism. In the introduction, Levi defines sorcery:

> For this science . . . there is nothing impossible, it commands the elements, knows the language of the stars and directs the planetary courses; when it speaks, the moon falls blood-red from heaven; the dead rise in their graves and mutter ominous words, as the night wind blows through their skulls. Mistress of love or of hate, occult science can dispense paradise or hell at its pleasure to human hearts; it disposes of all forms and confers beauty or ugliness; with the wand of [the Greek goddess] Circe it changes men into brutes and animals alternately into men; it disposes even of life and death, can confer wealth on its adepts [skilled practitioners].[15]

Levi wrote several influential books on high magic in the 1860s, and his words redefined sorcery for a new generation. He melded concepts from ancient Egypt, the Old Testament, and texts written during the early centuries AD that drew upon classical Greek mythology and Christian religious philosophy. The result was a new theory of sorcery that blended humans and gods into one powerful entity.

Levi said there is no wall of separation between an individual and the cosmic deities. Therefore the divine light can flow from human hands. However, the sorcerer must perform various ceremonies to command this natural light. In addition, the mind must be trained to see and understand the light. As Levi explains in grand terms:

"The sorcerer's
howlings were
heard from afar,
and belated
travelers imagined
that legions of
phantoms rose out
of the earth."

—Sorcerer Eliphas
Levi describing the
cacophony of a black
magic ceremony.

If your mind be perfectly free from all prejudice, superstition and incredulity [skepticism], you will rule spirits. If you do not obey blind forces, they will obey you. If you be wise like Solomon, you will perform the works of Solomon; if you be holy like Christ, you will accomplish the works of Christ. . . . To command the elements, we must have overcome their hurricanes, their lightnings, their abysses, their tempests. In order to DARE we must KNOW; in order to WILL, we must DARE; we must WILL to possess empire.[16]

"The Contagion of Madness"

Levi wrote that all sorcerers should have clear motives and good reasons to conduct a ceremony. Those that were conducted for dark purposes or foolish reasons could be dangerous to the sorcerer. Trouble could come to anyone who evoked the names of evil demons such as Satan or Beelzebub during a ceremony. This was considered not only dangerous but a waste of time. According to Levi, Satan was not powerful but a diminished apparition, the "most degraded and the least intelligent and feeblest"[17] of all spirits.

While condemning black magic, Levi provides some examples taken from the *Grand Grimoire*, a text said to be written around 1555. The book describes sorcerers who stole bodies from tombs to create philters, or magical potions, from the fat and blood of the recently deceased. This ghastly slime was combined with poisonous mushrooms, the toxic root aconite, and the hallucinogenic plant belladonna. The mixture was cooked over fires stoked with human bones and fed with crucifixes stolen from churches. The philter was completed when the sorcerer added the dust of dried

The nineteenth-century occult author Eliphas Levi warned sorcerers to avoid dark magic, noting that those who evoke the name of Satan risk harm to themselves and others. Never one to be toyed with, Satan devours the damned in this detail from Fra Angelico's The Last Judgment *(c. 1431).*

toads and ashes of cremated bodies. During the black magic ceremony, the sorcerer rubbed the philter on his breast, temples, and hands before calling up the spirits of the dead in desolate graveyards. Levi illustrates the scene:

> [The sorcerer's] howlings were heard from afar, and belated travelers imagined that legions of

phantoms rose out of the earth. The very trees, in their eyes, assumed appalling shapes; fiery orbs gleamed in the thickets; frogs in the marshes seemed to echo mysterious words of the Sabbath with croaking voices. It was the magnetism of hallucination and the contagion of madness.[18]

During this ceremony, sorcerers might be possessed with superhuman powers that allowed them to tear up dirt from graves with their fingernails. Bones could then be dragged from the ground and used to make grotesque crosses. The grimoire instructs the sorcerer to scream out, "Let the dead rise from their tombs!"[19] and slowly pace 4,500 steps in a straight line down the road. The sorcerer is instructed to lie down as if in a coffin and call out three times the name of the spirit he wishes to contact. Levi finishes this description of black magic with a warning: "No doubt anyone who is mad enough and wicked enough to abandon himself to such operations is predisposed to all chimeras and all phantoms. Hence the recipe of the Grand Grimoire is most [effective], but we advise none of our readers to test it."[20]

Scrying with a Speculatrix

Levi described ceremonial sorcery during an era when there was a great interest in the occult and spiritualism in the United States and Europe. People conducted séances in their living rooms to talk to dead relatives. Hundreds of people claimed to be mediums—people who possess the ability to communicate with the dead.

Tarot cards, which were first used to predict the future in the fourteenth century, became popular in the nineteenth century. Tarot decks contain 78 highly illustrated cards, each containing

Seeing with a Spirit

During scrying ceremonies, Frederick Hockley used a young woman as a seer to interpret the words allegedly made visible in a magic mirror by spirits. In the following excerpt from Hockley's notebook, he describes what occurred during scrying ceremonies:

> The writing which is seen in the mirror is done by the Spirit forming the letters in his mind as each word passes through his mind, so they take form of a reality and appear. The Seer who sees and the Spirit through whose mind these ideas pass are for the time one [being], but they are united by so slight a cord that the least thought jars it. When [the cord] is joined the writing appears small and when severed the writing disappears until the bond is again completed. [The seers] see with the Spirit's eyes and they read what is impressed upon the Spirit's mind.

Frederick Hockley, *The Rosicrucian Seer: The Magical Writings of Frederick Hockley*, ed. John Hamill. Wellingborough, UK: Aquarian, 1986, p. 112.

symbols. The cards have long been used for cartomancy, the practice of divination by cards. During this magical process, the sorcerer deals random cards from the tarot deck and divines meaning from the symbols on the cards. For example, if the Magician card appears, it predicts that wisdom, power, skill, and intelligence will rule a situation. If the Devil card is drawn, the future might include hatred, black magic, violence, or bizarre experiences.

Another ancient technique of sorcery, called scrying, was revived in London by Frederick Hockley, born in 1808. Scyring involves intensely gazing into crystals or mirrors until a celestial spirit guide appears. By the 1860s Hockley was well known among occultists for his work with crystals and what he called magic mirrors. These mirrors were consecrated in sorcery ceremonies for the specific purpose of scrying.

"It is an indispensible system of mystical advancement intended to raise the practitioner beyond the material and into the angelic and divine worlds."
—Occult expert P.G. Maxwell-Stuart describing the Kabbalah.

Hockley was an inventive scholar of sorcery, but he did not feel that he had sufficient magical powers to summon the celestial spirits. After studying scrying techniques from ancient Greece, Hockley concluded that adolescents, because of their pure hearts, were more gifted as seers. In the early 1850s Hockley tested his theory by conducting scrying ceremonies with a 13-year-old girl named Emma Louisa Leigh. To describe Leigh's role in the proceedings, he used the term *speculatrix*, a Latin word that means "a female observer or watcher."

During ceremonies with Leigh, Hockley carefully tried to avoid calling up evil spirits. To begin the sorcery, he invoked the name of Jesus three times to summon spirit guides. During the spells, Leigh allegedly saw letters and words forming before her as she peered intently into a magic mirror or crystal. Hockley sat beside her and wrote down what she saw.

Despite Hockley's precautions, evil spirits appeared on occasion. In July 1880, without the aid of a speculatrix, Hockley was scrying by staring into a common bottle of water. Before his eyes the water turned into a thick, dirty-red liquid before clearing again. A distorted spirit figure appeared in the bottle, human-like but with a long tail and strangely shaped horns. The spirit grew in size to fill the entire bottle. The alarmed Hockley reached first for a cork, then a heavy book, to prevent the spirit from rising out of the bottle. He was helpless against its strength.

As the horns rose out of the bottle, Hockley smashed it on the floor. This only allowed the spirit to continue growing until it was as large as a man. Hockley describes what happened next:

> I asked him what he wanted. He asked me to test his power by naming anything I desired, and said that if I found that he gave it to me and if I would promise him obedience, he would do the same in all other things. I resolutely told him that I would not—that had I known he was evil and could escape from the bottle I would not have called him; still he did not leave, and then I felt the place to be insufferable, so oppressive as to be almost suffocating. . . . The [spirit] rose above the carpet, the words disappeared, and there only remained a little piece of cold congealed blood: this I removed. In an adjoining room I . . . threw away the pieces of bottle, and determined to be more cautious in future.[21]

A Magical University for Sorcerers

The magical techniques described by Hockley and Levi provided a basis for the Golden Dawn. This organization was essentially a magical university for sorcerers. The Golden Dawn was founded by William Woodman, William Westcott, and Samuel Mathers in London in 1888. The three men had all studied under Levi. Mathers was multilingual, able to speak and write English, French, Latin, Greek, Hebrew, and Egyptian Coptic. He used his abilities to read and translate ancient magical texts into English. During this process, Mathers synthesized the occult knowledge he discovered in old grimoires into a coherent system of ceremonial sorcery.

The Golden Dawn system of sorcery was based on a series of 60 papers called the Cipher Manuscripts, written in a complex code previously developed in Germany in the 1500s. The manuscripts contain a series of convoluted initiation ceremonies and sorcery lessons for those wishing to join the order of the Golden Dawn. The founders of the Golden Dawn claimed the papers were ancient writings found among Hockley's possessions after his death in 1885. Others claim they were written by Woodman and Mathers and passed off as ancient knowledge to give the Golden Dawn credibility.

Whatever the source of the Cipher Manuscripts, by the mid-1890s the Golden Dawn had attracted over 100 members recruited from nearly every level of English society. The order had an unusual policy for the time—it was committed to treating men and women as equals. As the leading spokesperson for the Golden Dawn, Israel Regardie, wrote in 1937:

> [The membership] was represented by dignified professions as well as by all arts and sciences, to make but little mention of the trades and business

occupations. It included physicians, psychologists, clergymen, artists, and philosophers. And normal men and women, humble and unknown, from every walk of life [drew] inspiration from its font of wisdom, and undoubtedly many would be happy to recognize and admit the enormous debt they owe to it.[22]

Tarot cards, long a tool of sorcerers attempting to predict the future, became popular in the United States and Europe in the 1800s. Each illustrated card contains symbols that have particular meanings.

Golden Dawn sorcerers in training included many celebrities of the day, such as actress Florence Farr and renowned authors William Butler Yeats and Bram Stoker, creator of the horror novel *Dracula*. However, the order was cloaked in mystery and secrecy, and members were obliged to remain silent about their connection to the organization.

The classes at the Golden Dawn school of sorcery were extremely difficult. Students listened to long lectures and read thick grimoires and cryptic philosophy books filled with magical gibberish. They even had homework assignments and took tests. After successful completion of the lessons, the sorcerers were ceremonially initiated into various grades of three succeeding orders. Those who moved through the six grades of the First Order were considered to be adept at astrology, tarot card divinity, and geomancy, a type of earth magic. Geomancy involves predicting the future by throwing handfuls of stones, dirt, or sand on the ground. The patterns that are formed are interpreted to fit with a series of predetermined answers.

"Angelic and Divine Worlds"

The most important subject learned by sorcerers of the Golden Dawn concerns the Kabbalah (also spelled "Qabalah"). This complicated mystical system, nearly impossible for most to comprehend, was developed by Jewish mystics around the seventh century. P.G. Maxwell-Stuart describes the Kabbalah as "an indispensable system of mystical advancement intended to raise the practitioner beyond the material and into the angelic and divine worlds."[23]

The Kabbalah is based on a diagram called a Tree. The levels of the Tree illustrate how God created the universe by sending an emanation of himself into the void. The original emanation sent another emanation, which sent out another, until 10 existed. This group of emanations is called *sephiroth*, and they are connected to one another by 22 paths, each represented by a letter in the Hebrew alphabet.

Members of the Golden Dawn learned a wide variety of occult practices in a school of sorcery that had no equal at the time. In the modern era it could be compared to the fictional Hogwarts School of Witchcraft and Wizardry in the best-selling Harry Potter series. As Maxwell-Stuart writes, Harry Potter is "not a full-blown magical adept but a pupil, a status which presupposes that magic consists of techniques capable of being taught. . . . [Like members of the Golden Dawn] Potter and his friends, according to this definition, are sorcerers who apply their lessons to the suspension of natural law."[24]

"Do What Thou Wilt"

The English writer Aleister Crowley is one of the most notorious graduates of the Golden Dawn. Born into an extremely wealthy family in 1875, Crowley inherited a large fortune that made it possible for him to spend his life practicing magic and writing about it.

Crowley immediately created controversy after being initiated into the order of the Golden Dawn in November 1898. He moved into a luxury apartment in London and set up two rooms, one to experiment with black magic, the other for white magic. Following the practices of ancient shamans, Crowley experimented with hallucinogenic mushrooms and other drugs in order to achieve states of magical consciousness. During this period Crowley started to use the Old English spelling "magick" to differentiate the occult practice of sorcery from the type of magic tricks performed by stage magicians.

Like the fictional Hogwarts School of Witchcraft and Wizardry made famous in J.K. Rowling's popular Harry Potter series, the Golden Dawn, founded in 1888, trained sorcerers in the ways of magic. Hogwarts is pictured in this scene from the 2001 movie version of Harry Potter and the Sorcerer's Stone.

In 1904 Crowley had a life-changing experience while visiting the Great Pyramids of Giza in Egypt. He was conducting a ceremony to conjure up spirits of the air called sylphs. His wife, Rose, who knew little about ancient history, entered into a trance and told him the Egyptian god Horus was waiting for him. Crowley performed invocations to Horus for two weeks until, he claimed, the god's messenger, Aiwass, appeared. The messenger spoke in a series of poetic verses for three days, and Crowley wrote down every word. The spirit communications were eventually published in *The Book of the Law*, one of the most influential magical texts of the modern era.

In *The Book of the Law*, Crowley announces he is a prophet of a new age called the Aeon of Horus. He defines sorcery as the art and science of using one's determination, or willpower, to bend and shape the world to one's desires. According to Crowley, the law of magic is using the power of the will, or, "Do what thou wilt shall be the whole of the law. . . . There is no law beyond do what thou wilt."[25]

The Wickedest Man in the World

In 1907 Crowley founded a new order of sorcery called Thelema, from the Greek word meaning will, wish, or purpose. In the years that followed, he wrote a series of books called *The Holy Books of Thelema*, which he claimed were dictated to him by Aiwass. The numerous texts are filled with complex magical ceremonies that involve astrology, tarot cards, and Eastern practices such as mediation and yoga. Believing himself to be the greatest sorcerer alive, Crowley founded a magical society based on the Golden Dawn. He named it Argenteum Astrum—the Silver Star. After founding the order, Crowley attracted hundreds of members through a journal called *Equinox*, published biannually.

Crowley, already a controversial figure, began writing about conducting magical ceremonies that involved sex and drugs. This attracted the attention of critics, who called Crowley a pervert, a lunatic, a black magician, and a fraud. He was widely referred to in the British press as the "Wickedest Man in the World." Despite his bizarre exploits and the publicity that followed, Crowley eventually condemned the practice of black magic. As he wrote in a 1933 newspaper article:

> To practice black magic you have to violate every principle of science, decency and intelligence.

You must be obsessed with an insane idea of the importance of the petty object of your wretched and selfish desires. I have been accused of being a "black magician." No more foolish statement was ever made about me. I despise the thing to such an [extent] that I can hardly believe the existence of people so debased and idiotic as to practice it.[26]

Crowley died in 1954, but his books remain in print and have influenced generations of sorcerers. His 1911 work *Magick (Book 4)*, also called *Magick in Theory and Practice*, contains detailed descriptions of the necessary tools and methods for conducting ceremonial magic. Like many sorcerers, ancient and modern, Crowley thrived on attention. By titillating the public, Crowley sold more books, attracted more disciples, and ensured that he would be remembered long after his death. Crowley, Levi, and the magicians of the Golden Dawn spent their lives trying to bend the natural world to their will. While their ceremonial sorcery remains controversial, it has become an accepted part of occult practice and remains a force in the New Age world of modern magic.

CHAPTER 3

Charms, Potions, and Powders

The sorcerer's craft relies on the use of various herbs, gems, minerals, and other items that are believed to possess power of some sort. Foods such as apple seeds, lemon juice, and vanilla are thought to possess the power of love, so they are used in potions to attract romance. Reptile bones, cactus needles, and dead scorpions are said to possess evil magic and might be conjured into a powder meant to sicken a victim. And a cloth or wax doll made in the shape of an enemy purportedly has the magical power to cause death if it is symbolically drowned or burned.

The Powers of Elements, Planets, and Colors

Parts of vegetables, bushes, trees, flowers, and other plants are all categorized as herbs by sorcerers and are seen as having natural magical powers. Other magical items include stones and precious metals. Skillful sorcerers can draw on the innate powers in these

Every natural
substance is said
to be ruled by one
of the four basic
elements—earth,
air, fire, or water.

things to make spells stronger. The basis for this belief is that every natural substance is said to be ruled by one of the four basic elements—earth, air, fire, or water. In the lore of sorcery, these ruling elements are the building blocks of the universe and are associated with supernatural forces.

Each element is thought to have its own specific powers. Earth represents stability and permanence. Water is the opposite, promoting volatility and change. Air is seen as a gas that aids in movement, mobility, travel, and communication. The fire element is said to have the power to transform, turning water into air and earth into liquid.

Astrology is also used to classify various herbs, gems, and minerals, and each item is linked to the sun, moon, or planets. This purportedly provides substances with specific magical powers that help the sorcerer carry out successful spells. For example, the daffodil is ruled by the planet Venus, named after the Roman goddess of love and beauty. Wiccan herbalist Paul Beyerl describes the magical aspects of plants associated with Venus:

> [Herbs of Venus] often have with them the energy which increases our ability to attract those things we desire. They are best used in this manner to attract imagery such as sought by artists, musicians, and others involved in the creative arts. . . . They also increase psychic perception, opening our awareness to many other senses. They have been used successfully by those who work on the astral plane.[27]

The ruling element of the daffodil is water, which can bring change to a static situation. These associations give the daffodil

"By the Virtue of the Elements"

The *Grimorium Verum*, or *Grimoire of Truth*, was published in Rome in 1517. The author, known as Alibeck the Egyptian, brings together God, the stars, the elements, and other magical substances in a spell meant to conjure powerful spirits:

> I conjure thee . . . by the authority of our Father God Almighty, by the virtues of Heaven and by the Stars, by the virtue of the Angels, and by the virtue of the Elements, by the virtues of the stones and herbs, and of snow-storms, winds and thunder: that thou now obtain all the necessary power into thyself for the pefectioning of the achievement of those things in which we are at present concerned! And this without deception, untruth, or anything of that nature whatsoever, by God the Creator of the Sun of Angels! Amen. Then we recite the Seven Psalms, and afterwards the following words:
>
> Dalmaley lamekh cadat pancia velous merroe lamideck caldurech anereton mitraton: Most Pure Angels, be the guardians of these instruments, they are needed for many things.

Alibeck the Egyptian, *Grimorium Verum*, Hermetics Resource Site, 2009. www.hermetics.org.

magical abilities to attract romance and increase fertility. A sorcerer searching for love might wear a daffodil close to the heart.

Like other gemstones, the garnet is ruled by planets and elements. It is associated with fire and the planet Mars, named after the Roman god of war. These classifications imbue the stone with magical powers to enhance strength and endurance. New Age author Scott Cunningham describes the magical associations of garnet: "[The] garnet is worn for protective purposes. Five hundred years ago it was thought to drive off demons and night phantoms. Today, the garnet . . . [is seen to] create a shield of highly charged positive vibrations which repels negative energies upon contact."[28]

Protecting a Person from Trouble

Astrology and the elements play important roles in each item used in magical spells. This is particularly true when sorcerers create an amulet, or magical charm. The term *amulet* is from the Latin word *amuletum*, which means "an object that protects a person from trouble." Other words for *amulet* include *charm* and *talisman*. Ancient pagans wore necklaces of animal teeth, claws, bones, and feathers to ensure successful hunts. The Romans wore carvings of a hand with an open palm, a symbol said to ward off evil.

Sorcerers also recognize the powers of amulets and have used them for supernatural purposes all over the world. A magical talisman might consist of a potent symbol like a pentagram or mystical words from a grimoire. Sorcerers can also carry out spells by combining herbs, stones, and other objects into a small pouch worn around the neck. Native Americans call these amulets medicine bags. African sorcerers and voodoo practitioners call them gris-gris bags. Other names for *gris-gris bags* include *conjure bags, mojo bags, ouanga bags*, or simply *charm bags*.

The Shower of Gold

A gris-gris bag is created with specific items with magical powers over love, passion, money, luck, success, health, protection from evil, spiritual development, sickness, or cursing an enemy. Ceremonial magic is used in the creation of the gris-gris bag. New Orleans native Ray T. Malbrough practices hoodoo, an American form of voodoo that incorporates Native American, African American, and European magical concepts. Malbrough explains how the intentions of the sorcerer give a gris-gris bag its power:

> It has been said thoughts are things. Human thought produces energy, and the energy creates the force which in turn produces action. . . . Thus your thoughts, always guided and controlled by your will, become a force that neither time nor distance can deter. All your thoughts, therefore, produce a mental vibration that cannot be lost. In making a gris-gris bag, a certain thought pattern is created and put into motion.[29]

When a sorcerer makes a gris-gris bag, he or she conducts a magic ritual, lighting candles, burning incense, and anointing the forehead with herbal oil. Each of these items, however, must be chosen specially for its magical powers. For a spell meant to attract money, the sorcerer might use a green candle. A potion called money-drawing oil would be made from olive oil infused with aromatic herbs such as myrrh, frankincense, and sandalwood, ingredients associated with riches. The sorcerer could also create shower of gold incense for the ritual, combining cinnamon, bayberry, and other herbs. The final item for the spell, a small cloth pouch for the gris-gris bag, would be green in color.

Did You Know?

Sorcerers believe the symbolic drowning or burning of a cloth or wax doll made in the shape of an enemy can cause that person's death.

During the ritual, the sorcerer assembles the gris-gris bag while clearly visualizing, or envisioning, the outcome produced by the spell. The sorcerer might picture a large pile of $100 bills, a handful of diamonds, or a treasure chest full of jewels and gold. These thoughts purportedly send out vibrations that attract the desired objects.

While visualizing riches, the sorcerer might place small amounts of what are said to be money-drawing herbs and stones and other items into the gris-gris bag. Specific items for a money-drawing gris-gris bag include coins, the herbs buckeye, five-finger grass, and silverweed, and a magnetic mineral called a lodestone. A special magical substance, called money-drawing powder, made from various herbs and spices, is also added. According to Malbrough, the sorcerer chants the following words while assembling the charm:

> The lodestones attract to me, money which I see.
> Buckeye, five-finger grass, giving aid which will last,
> Money drawing powder and silver weed,
> Bringing me money, which I need.[30]

Once it is assembled, the gris-gris bag is ready to work its magic. The money-drawing bag might be kept in the wallet, purse, pocket, wall safe, or bank deposit box. A gris-gris bag for love would be pinned inside the clothing, worn around the waist, or around the neck and close to the heart.

Poppets and Voodoo Dolls

Sorcerers most often create gris-gris bags for positive outcomes, but they can also be used for black magic. Bags created for cursing purposes are hung in trees or bushes near the front door of

Black magic is not condoned in Haitian voodoo practice. But a voodoo doll (such as this one from Haiti) might be used by other sorcerers to torture or kill a person. To be effective it must contain something from the intended victim—such as a toenail, hair strand, sweat, saliva or urine.

an enemy's house. Harmful energies from gris-gris bags purportedly infect the intended victims whenever they pass by them. Another type of powerful black magic comes in the form of a doll meant to represent a person.

In classical Greece, magic dolls were called *kolossoi* and were

Did You Know?

The term *amulet* is from the Latin word *amuletum,* which means "an object that protects a person from trouble."

made from lead, bronze, or silver. In Europe they are called poppets and in the United States, voodoo dolls. However, the American term is misleading because the Haitian voodoo religion does not condone black magic.

Poppets are made of wood, wax, clay, or rags. It is said that the power of a doll is enhanced if it contains something from the targeted victim's body, such as toenails, hair, sweat, saliva, or urine. A picture of the victim's face may even be cut out and pasted on the doll's head.

When the sorcerer creates a doll during a ritual, he makes it the focus of malevolent thoughts. When it is finished, the sorcerer tortures the doll, and the pain is purportedly transferred to the victim. A doll might be twisted, burned, tied, or pierced with nails or animal fangs and claws. Each method has a different effect. A nail placed in the doll's mouth insures a witness to a crime will remain silent. To prevent success, the name of the victim is stuffed into a slit in the back of a doll along with cayenne pepper. Then the doll's hands are sewn together and it is blindfolded and placed in a kneeling position in an out-of-the-way corner. As long as the doll remains there, the enemy will be unsuccessful in life. Turning the doll's head backward from the body creates mental confusion. Hacking the doll apart purportedly causes death.

"Heavy Damages"

In centuries past the use of poppets for black magic was thought to be quite dangerous. A doll might be captured by the victim and used against the sorcerer in what is known as countermagic. In such cases the torturer becomes the tortured. There are more modern problems associated with doll sorcery, according to Wiccan author Paul Huson:

"[Should] one of your wax voodoo dolls be brought into court and shown as sufficient evidence of your practice of . . . intimidation upon the intended victim, you could find yourself in trouble with a lawsuit on your hands and heavy damages awarded against you."[31]

Some may laugh at the idea of suing the maker of a voodoo doll. However, in 2008 a Paris company began selling a voodoo doll in the image of French president Nicolas Sarkozy. It was sold with 12 pins and a booklet with instructions on putting a curse on the president. Sarkozy filed a lawsuit to prevent the sale of the doll. He claimed the product was an abuse of his image. The French court rejected his case, and publicity from the lawsuit quickly made the Sarkozy voodoo doll a best-selling item.

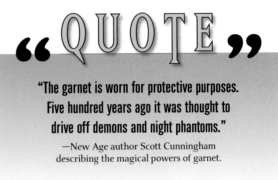

"The garnet is worn for protective purposes. Five hundred years ago it was thought to drive off demons and night phantoms."

—New Age author Scott Cunningham describing the magical powers of garnet.

"Toil and Trouble"

In past centuries kings and queens truly feared curses by witches, who were often referred to as sorcerers. In 1590 King James VI of Scotland believed witches tried to kill him by melting a wax effigy in his image. In another incident, James accused witches of trying to drown him by calling up a storm while he was at sea. It was believed that evil witches could cause extreme weather conditions by creating mini storms in their cauldrons with magical ingredients. Perhaps the playwright William Shakespeare had this in mind when he wrote *Macbeth* around 1603.

In one of the most well-known scenes in *Macbeth*, three witches conjure up a potion with the words "Double, double

The three witches of William Shakespeare's Macbeth *mix together all sorts of gruesome ingredients to make their potion in this 1905 illustration. In Shakespeare's time, it was thought that sorcerers and witches created deadly potions.*

toil and trouble; Fire burn and cauldron bubble." In what Shakespeare calls the "charmed pot," witches "boil and bake"[32] a disgusting mixture. It is made from the filet of a snake, the eye of a newt, the toe of a frog, the wool of a bat, and the tongue of a dog. After adding a lizard's leg and an owl's wing, the potion becomes even more ghastly. A human nose, lips, and liver are added along with baby fingers.

In Shakespeare's time it was widely believed that witches created such potions. Shakespeare is said to have taken the spell from a real grimoire. And the magic books published during that era often contained horrid methods for concocting potions. Sorcerers were instructed to create deadly substances from snake venom, amphibian parts, and saps from poisonous plants and fungi. They fed frogs and snakes highly toxic plants like foxglove and hemlock. After the creatures died they were dried near a fire. According to Eliphas Levi, the ashes of these pitiful creatures would "cause any person who may have a pinch of it mixed with his drink to grow wilted and old, and subsequently to die amidst horrible sufferings, or in a state of complete collapse."[33]

"The Composition of Death"

Whether such a potion would actually have killed a person is unknown. Even so, it would have commanded a high price from those wishing to frighten, harass, or harm their foes. And some recipes were truly deadly. A formula from the 1555 *Grand Grimoire* called "The Composition of Death" contains a detailed recipe that consists of boiling highly noxious nitric acid and arsenic in a cauldron along with sawdust from oak bark, rose water, and other ingredients. The resulting drink, with the power to dissolve an iron nail, would instantly kill anyone who consumed it.

Those who created poisons and powders were said to have sold their souls to the devil. Levi, who worked positive magic, criticized malevolent magicians for giving sorcery a bad name:

> The [evil] sorcerer and sorceress were almost invariably a species of human toad, swollen with long-enduring rancors [ill will]. They were poor, repulsed by all and consequently full of hatred. The

"The color of it
was like saffron in
powder but heavy
and shining like
pounded glass."

—Alchemist and
medical doctor Jean
Baptista van Helmont
describing the
Philosopher's Stone.

fear which they inspired was their consolation and their revenge; poisoned themselves by a society [in] which they had experienced nothing but the rebuffs and the vices, they poisoned in their turn all those who were weak enough to fear them, and avenged upon beauty and youth their accursed old age and their atrocious ugliness. . . . That human souls could descend to such an abyss of crime and madness must assuredly astonish and afflict us.[34]

The Philosopher's Stone

Educated sorcerers like Levi did not create poisons and poppets. Instead they pursued a higher calling through their studies of chemistry, biology, philosophy, and mysticism. Their goal was the practice of alchemy, or the ability to transform lead into silver or gold. The key to alchemy, according to ideas introduced in the tenth century, was a magical substance called the Philosopher's Stone. Because it consisted of fine particles, this substance was not really a stone but a powder. For this reason the Philosopher's Stone was sometimes referred to by sorcerers as the powder of projection.

The strength of the Philosopher's Stone was based on the now-discredited belief that all matter is composed of identical atoms. The Philosopher's Stone was believed to have the power to rearrange the atoms of one substance and thereby change it into another substance. For example, the atoms of lead could be regrouped to make gold.

While the desire for gold was strong, the quest for the Philosopher's Stone went beyond satisfying the greed of the sorcerer. It was thought that the Philosopher's Stone could also rearrange the atoms in the human body. This would heal the sick and prolong life indefinitely. By pursuing the Philosopher's Stone, alchemists sought immortality.

"The Most Pure Gold"

The search for a formula for the Philosopher's Stone consumed the lives of innumerable sorcerers. One of the earliest descriptions of the substance comes from 1618. In *De Natura Vitae Eternae* (*The Nature of Eternal Life*), the alchemist and medical doctor Jean Baptista van Helmont writes: "I have seen and I have

Well-schooled sorcerers pursued a higher calling than creating poisons and poppets. They devoted themselves to the practice of alchemy, which involved the transformation of lead into silver or gold. A 1935 illustration depicts an alchemist at work as he tries to make gold.

touched the Philosopher's Stone more than once. The color of it was like saffron in powder but heavy and shining like pounded glass. I had once given me the fourth of a grain, and I [combined it] with . . . eight ounces of quicksilver [mercury] heated in a crucible. The result of the projection was eight ounces . . . of the most pure gold."[35]

Although Van Helmont did not provide a specific formula for the Philosopher's Stone, he claimed to have received it from a man known as Butler, an Irish sorcerer known for providing magical cures. In one experiment, Van Helmont and Butler mixed the Philosopher's Stone with olive oil. This was rubbed on the forehead and tongue of an aged woman who suffered from depression, paralyzed fingers, and a swollen arm. According to alchemical lore, these maladies, which the woman had had for 18 years, miraculously disappeared.

Butler said he learned to make the Philosopher's Stone after being captured by African pirates and sold as a slave in Arabia. His Arabian master was an alchemist who showed him how to conjure the red powder. Butler escaped captivity and brought the Philosopher's Stone to Belgium, where he purportedly gave some to Van Helmont.

Gold at Fort Knox

In the late nineteenth century an alchemist named Stephen H. Emmens claimed to have created a new metal called argentaurum gold with the use of a Philosopher's Stone. In 1897 Emmens conjured this metal, which was almost pure gold. According to an 1899 article in the *New York Herald*, Emmens sold the ingots to the US Mint, which manufactures coins. Instead of working with lead, Emmens claimed to have rearranged the molecules in silver to create the gold in a secret process.

Regardless of whether Emmens actually accomplished this feat, he died shortly after he invented the process. His alchemical secrets died with him, but the mysterious argentaurum gold still exists. Author and paranormal researcher Vincent H. Gaddis contends that Emmens's argentaurum is stored with the government's gold supply at Fort Knox, Kentucky.

Nature's Magic

From alchemy to voodoo dolls, the supernatural work of sorcerers has long been based in the natural world where each herb, gem, and metal has purported magical powers. Practicing sorcerers continue to believe that the forces of nature can add magical power to their daily lives. Earthquakes, hurricanes, volcanoes, and tidal waves unleash the furious capacities of earth, air, fire, and water. For believers, anything might be possible if these powers can be harnessed in a charm, potion, or powder.

CHAPTER 4

Summoning the Dead

People in modern New Orleans can visit Marie Laveau's House of Voodoo to purchase items used in sorcery. Laveau's sells wands, candles, incense, oils, and charms used in voodoo spells to attract love or money, inflict pain on enemies, or even to achieve a favorable outcome in court. The store is among dozens in New Orleans that profit from a widespread fascination with voodoo rituals, which originated in Haiti in the eighteenth century.

Practitioners of voodoo often interact with the spirits of the dead. During voodoo ceremonies worshippers believe the dead enter their bodies, take possession of them, and speak through their mouths. During this time, the spirits offer advice, reveal secrets, and grant favors. One of the supreme spirits of voodoo, named Ghede, is the ruler of death, destruction, and the end of time. He dresses in black, wears a top hat, and lingers at the crossroads of death where all living beings must one day travel. Ghede acts as an intermediary between the living and the dead, guiding newly deceased souls into the afterlife. During voodoo rituals, worshippers get in touch with Ghede through a potion made from rum and extremely hot habenero peppers. Voodooists drink or rub the mixture on their bodies, writhing in pain as they inquire about their own impending deaths or the spirits of relatives who have already died.

Voodoo is among many belief systems that are based on communication with the spirits of the dead. This activity is called necromancy. It involves rituals to raise the spirits of the dead so they can be used to control the present and change the future.

The Past, the Future, and the Dead

The idea that spirits are wise and possess information not available to the living is a basic tenet of sorcery. Sorcerers believe spirits know where a treasure might be hidden, which side will prevail in a war, or when death will strike. Professor of ancient history Daniel Ogden explains why the dead have long been seen by sorcerers as the best sources for such information:

> The dead could impart the wisdom of their own experiences, particularly of those that led to their own death. The dead in their graves could witness all that went on around them. The [gathering] of the dead in the underworld pooled their knowledge and understanding of all things. The roots of the future lay in the past, so that the people of one's past were better able to perceive one's future. The future itself was prepared in the underworld. . . . Souls detached from their encumbered bodies had

a clearer perception of all things and processes. Perhaps [the spirits] also drew some power from the fertile earth itself.[36]

The Latin variation of the word *necromancy* means "divination through the dead." To practice necromancy, sorcerers called nec-

Haitians pay their respects to the dead through rituals involving Ghede, the spirit of death, and a potion made from rum and hot peppers. A worshipper dressed as Ghede holds the homemade potion during a ceremony at a cemetery in Port-au-Prince.

romancers venture into the shadowy world located somewhere between life and death. In this mystical dimension, it is believed the dead are half alive while the necromancer steps closer to death. Eliphas Levi describes the ritualized death and rebirth of the necromancer: "To behold these strange forms we must put ourselves in an abnormal condition akin to sleep or death; in other words, we must magnetize ourselves and enter into a kind of lucid and waking [state of sleep]."[37]

Over the centuries various magical spells, rituals, and other practices evolved that allowed the sorcerer to break down the walls between the living and the dead. To traverse the boundary between life and death was not something to be taken lightly. It required great thought, dedication, and deliberation by the sorcerer.

Light and Darkness

The earliest grimoires written about necromancy were created in classical Greece. During this time, the average Greek citizen believed the spirits of the dead were everywhere. They might be perceived as wispy shadows, breaths of air, tiny winged creatures, rotten corpses, or figures in dreams. Those who appeared in human form had the ability to eat, drink, and even make love.

The spirits of the dead could be placed in several different categories. Some were dead relatives who looked after their living families and took care of their needs. A second type of spirit was manifested from people who were wicked in life and were being punished by the gods in death. These ghosts were forced to wander in a bleak netherworld between life and death. A third manifestation, called larvae, was described by Roman authors in the early centuries AD. These creatures had skeleton bodies and hideous facial features. Larvae were not only troublesome

"QUOTE"

"The [gathering] of the dead in the underworld pooled their knowledge and understanding of all things."

—Professor of ancient history Daniel Ogden on why necromancers attempt communication with the dead.

to the living, they also tortured the dead in the underworld.

Whatever their form, the dead were available for consultation through necromancy. If a person experienced bad luck or illness, he or she would likely assume that the troubles were caused by spirits of the dead. A necromancer would be consulted to call up the spirits, which would be petitioned for good luck, health, love, or riches. The necromancer could also direct the spirits to harm or kill an enemy. As Levi writes: "There are two kinds of Necromancy, that of light and that of darkness—the evocation [of the dead] by Prayer, Pentacle and Perfumes, and the evocation by blood, imprecations and sacrilege [curses and disrespect]. We . . . advise no one to devote themselves to the second."[38]

"The Carcasses of the Slain"

The methods of necromancy developed by the early Greeks and Romans survived for centuries with little variation, and the purpose of talking to the dead remained the same in every era. Spirits were thought to meet with the necromancer and take his soul to the netherworld. The spirits granted the sorcerer special powers to see the dead both in the real world and in the mystical phantom world. During this initial process, the necromancer attempted to bond with the spirit in a mutual friendship so that the spirit would be readily available in the future. Once the bonding was complete, the necromancer awakened tired and drained. At this time, however, the sorcerer considered himself twice born, a citizen of both the real world and the ghostly netherworld.

Throughout the centuries, most people have considered necromancy to be a morbid, gory black art. Necromancers were viewed as Satanic. They were often accused of visiting graveyards on full moon nights to dig up corpses, and such charges have a basis in reality. Necromancers believe that the spirits of the dead are more active around graves, cemeteries, battlefields, execution grounds, and other scenes of violence. According to sixteenth-century writer Heinrich Cornelius Agrippa, necromancy "worketh all its experiments by the carcasses of the slain, and their bones and members, and what is from them, because there is in these things a spiritual power friendly to them."[39]

Agrippa's books influenced English sorcerers John Dee and Edward Kelley, who practiced their dark arts sometime between 1581 and 1587. Dee was a well-known sorcerer who worked as an astrologer and scientific advisor for Queen Mary and her successor Queen Elizabeth in the mid-1500s. When he worked with Kelley, Dee acted as the magician who prayed and recited spells from Agrippa's books in order to bring up spirits. Kelley was a scryer who stared into a crystal ball during the ceremonies and spoke aloud the words he heard from the spirits.

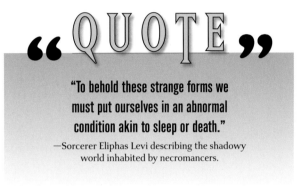

Visiting the Cemetery

Dee wrote detailed accounts of Kelley's conversations with the spirits during scrying rituals. According to Dee's diary, he visited a cemetery with Kelley late on a December night in 1581 to practice necromancy. Although there were no witnesses to back up Dee's claims, the sorcerer said that he was able to summon a dead man who rose bodily from his grave and walked toward him. Dee and Kelley were standing within a magic circle they had drawn on the ground that protected them from attack. The animated corpse came so close, however, that the sorcerers reported

Preparing to Summon a Spirit

In his pioneering book on ceremonial magic, *Dogme et Rituel de la Haute Magie*, Eliphas Levi described preparations a sorcerer should take to summon the spirit of a deceased friend or relative:

> We must collect, in the first place, carefully the memorials of him or her whom we desire to behold, the articles he used, and on which his impression remains; we must also prepare an apartment in which the person lived, or otherwise one of similar kind, and place his portrait veiled in white therein, surrounded with his favorite flowers, which must be renewed daily. A fixed date must then be chosen, being that of the person's birth, or one that was especially fortunate for his and our own affection. . . .
>
> Every evening at the same hour we must shut ourselves in the chamber consecrated to the memory of the lamented person, using only one small light. . . . [Finally], we should fumigate the apartment with a little good incense, and go out backwards. On the morning of the day fixed for the evocation, we should adorn ourselves as if for a festival . . . and one portion of . . . broken bread should be set aside; a little wine should be placed also in the glass of the person whom we design to invoke.

Eliphas Levi and A.E. Waite, *Dogme et Rituel de la Haute Magie, Part II: The Ritual of Transcendental Magic*. London: Rider, 1896, p. 75.

seeing its glassy eyes and sunken cheeks. Dee almost fainted but recovered enough to ask a few questions. The corpse identified itself by the name Anel and said all power, good and bad, was situated within him. Dee asked Anel where a hidden or buried treasure might be found, but this only irritated the spirit, who said, "Don't trouble yourself [with that]. These things are of no account."[40] Anel had little else to say other than telling Dee he now had the powers to summon the dead at will. In the aftermath of the event, Dee used that power repeatedly.

Several months after meeting Anel, Dee and Kelley claimed to have spoken with Michael, the archangel of the Bible who is viewed as the commander of God's army. After Michael appeared, Kelley and Dee spoke with hundreds of spirits of the dead. One was a small child in bloody garments with the letter *h* on his forehead. Another was a pretty girl, about eight years old, who said her name was Madimi. She could not tell the necromancers where she was from, she explained, or she would be beaten. After playing in a stack of books in Dee's room, Madimi terrified the sorcerers, telling them Satan was angry with Dee for summoning the spirits and wanted to kill him.

Enochian Magic

Most of the necromancy conducted by Dee and Kelley did not produce such frightening results. Instead, the spirits of the dead provided information about a new type of sorcery referred to as Enochian magic. This term is derived from Dee's claim that the biblical figure Enoch, Adam's great-grandson, was the last human who knew the magical language of the Enochian methods before Dee and Kelley revealed it.

The Enochian magical methods were revealed to Dee and Kelley over the course of 13 tedious months. Dee conjured up the dead, and the spirits revealed to Kelley an entirely unfamiliar alphabet consisting of 21 characters. In this manner the sorcerers wrote a long book, letter by letter. Some of the magical wisdom was presented in the form of pie charts, graphs, and complex tables. This tiresome task was further complicated because some words and entire sentences were spelled backward.

Enochian magic, as revealed to the necromancers, consists of three grimoires, *Liber Logaeth*, *De Heptarchia Mystica*, and *Claves Angelicae*. The books contain keys to the mysterious spirit alphabet, magical symbols, and spells to invoke the dead. Some pages are filled with nearly unpronounceable magic invocations such as: "Madriax ds praf lil chis micaolz saanir caosgo od fisis balzizras Iaida."[41]

In all, the three books of Enochian magic consist of about 250 such words, which were translated into English by Dee and others in later years. Much of the information, supposedly dictated by the dead, is sparse or ambiguous. As a result, countless other sorcerers have experimented with Enochian magic, attempting to clarify or expand on the information. The system forms the basis for the sorcery of the Golden Dawn. Necromancers from that order added substantially to Enochian grimoires.

Dee believed his magical knowledge was pure, revealed by God and the angels. As Dee wrote, he avoided "filthy abuse . . . [and] Spirituall creatures of the damned sort: angels of darknes, forgers & patrons of lies & untruths."[42] Whatever Dee's intentions, he was branded a witch and a black magician because of his necromancy. However, as a friend to Queen Elizabeth, he was protected and was not burned at the stake like many other sorcerers of the day. Today some of the artifacts used during the rituals, including several crystal balls and a gold amulet, are in the British Museum in London.

Soul Flight

When the spirits of the dead explained Enochian magic to Kelley, his moods often resembled those of a madman. During one of the sessions, Kelley stated, "My head is all on fire."[43] The pressure of conversing with the dead caused his moods to swing between hysteria, ecstasy, grief, and extreme apathy. Paul Huson explains why Kelley suffered:

> The summoning of the dead has always been considered by [sorcerers] as among some of the most dangerous operations in the book, strangely enough, sometimes even more so than the summoning of demons. . . . [The] nervous and physical depletion visited upon participants can prove truly onerous, and in some extremely rare cases, fatal.[44]

While most sorcerers try to avoid loosing their sanity during necromantic rituals, shamans in Peru deliberately induce states of ecstasy and madness. They do so by taking powerful hallucinogenic drugs and drumming, dancing, and singing for hours. This process allows shamans to achieve a state known as soul flight. In this condition the soul of the shaman purportedly leaves his or her body and travels to the spirit world, where communications take place with the dead.

Peruvian shamans called *curanderos*, or healers, have been practicing necromancy for hundreds of years. They use the psychoactive drug mescaline in a ritualistic manner during séances that can last up to 12 hours. While under the influence of the drug, the shaman is provided what is called a magical second sight or psychic sight.

During rituals, the shaman snorts a tobacco mixture into his nose, sprays perfumes on his clients and assistants, whistles, sings, shakes gourd rattles, and speaks lengthy invocations to the spirits. These actions take the shaman on a journey to the supernatural world inhabited by shadowy forces. During these ceremonies, shamans gain insight that allows them to destroy curses that have been placed on victims.

Opening Doors

In 1988 a curandero named Helmer Aguilar conducted a long healing ritual he called a charm. At the end, as the sun rose in the early morning, Aguilar found himself in a tunnel in the spirit world. It seemed to be about 9 feet (3m) in diameter with granite walls blackened by the smoke from innumerable candles. Aguilar felt he was being absorbed into the air and transported by a spirit down the tunnel into the heart of a mountain, where he found a castle. Aguilar described the trance state:

> It's a castle, a real castle, and one opens the main doors and inside there is a courtyard off of which you open smaller doors . . . like [a] labyrinth. . . . And you go along entering that charm. You have dominated it and you know where each small door is located, where each window is, where the ancients are located. You know what [spirit] animals come out because you dominate that charm and you have that charm, you know it like the palm of your hand.[45]

Once inside the castle, Aguilar had to knock on every door because each one led to a different room with a unique spirit. He purportedly spoke to the ghosts of the dead, and they instructed him to cure his patient through prescribed healing rituals and herbal folk medicines.

Aguilar later discovered that other curanderos had similar experiences in which they allegedly traveled down the tunnel to the castle. One healer used his guitar to play a song that transported him to the spirit rooms. Another used a gourd rattle filled with seeds. Each seed opened a door. Aguilar was able to use this information in later rituals, as he stated: "After that, upon sounding the rattle and moving each seed in the rattle those doors opened automatically."[46]

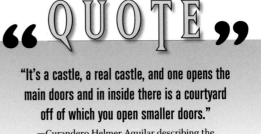

The Dumb Supper

Curanderos like Aguilar claim to speak to the dead through elaborate rituals. However, occultists have long believed that the dead can be summoned by serving them supper. The ceremony, called the dumb supper, can be used for two purposes. The necromancer can supposedly evoke a deceased relative for consultation or call up a spectral apparition known as a wraith. The second spirit will reveal the name of a future lover or spouse.

The term *dumb* in this case means *silent*, and the dumb supper can be traced back to the ancient Celts. The Celts were a tribal group that inhabited Ireland, Great Britain, and parts of France in the early centuries AD. In the autumn they celebrated a harvest festival called Samhain for three days. It was believed that the tissue that separated the living from the dead was thinnest on the last day of Samhain, around October 31, the date of the modern Halloween. On this day, the Celts feasted, danced, and sang with those who had died during the previous year.

Each year at the end of October the ancient Celts feasted (as depicted in this hand-colored woodcut), sang, and danced with those who had died the previous year. The celebrants donned costumes to confuse the spirits and thus prevent them from taking the living back to the land of the dead.

Although Samhain was celebrated with joy, the Celts were fearful that the spirits might take the living back to the land of the dead. In order to avoid this fate, they dressed in costumes. These disguises were thought to confuse the spirits. As another way to insure their safety, the Celts lit candles in every room of the house and set the table with fine food and drink, being sure to put out place settings for all members of the household, living and dead. The living then sat silently as the spirits enjoyed the meal. This evolved into the dumb suppers that are celebrated by occultists in modern times on Halloween.

The Melding of Minds

Preparations for the dumb supper can be very complex, involving rituals that take place for 13 days prior to the dinner. A shrine is built and covered with a dark cloth. A portrait of the dead person is placed on the shrine along with small personal items, such as jewelry or a favorite book. During this 13-day period, the necromancer lights incense each midnight, whispers the name of the deceased, and recalls shared moments of love and affection. Throughout this period, the necromancer remains apart from the living while focusing on the dead.

On the night of the evocation, the dining room table must be ritually set with a black tablecloth, dishes, napkins, and candles. Only two place settings are necessary, one for the necromancer and the other for the dead person's spirit. However, as Huson explains, "Every action in this ceremony must be performed silently and [while walking] backwards for only thus do we begin to walk in the paths of the dead."[47]

The favorite foods and drink of the deceased are served silently, with the necromancer walking backward to and from the kitchen the entire time. Once the table is set, the spirit is summoned in a silent invocation. The necromancer is instructed not to look at the chair that awaits the spirit. After the deceased's name is evoked three times, the loved one will purportedly arrive. The sorcerer can then speak with the spirit, as Huson explains:

[Most] witches find that this takes the form of a peculiar wordless communion, a sort of spiritual osmosis or blending together of ideas, your own, and that of the deceased. Even if [you do not see the spirit] . . . it can nevertheless be a very unnerving experience to find yourself confronted by someone loved, but long dead, and in such intimate contact again that your very minds meld together.[48]

Those who have conduced dumb suppers say the experience seems to pass very quickly and the spirit soon fades away. A silent prayer is offered at the end of the dumb supper, and the necromancer says goodbye.

Life, Death, and the Afterlife

The comedian George Carlin once said, "Life is a near-death experience."[49] Although he was making a joke, the truth behind his words has motivated necromancers for centuries. Life and death are inseparable and intertwined, and one would not exist without the other. While most people believe that death is permanent, some cannot accept the finality of mortality. For that reason, nearly every culture and religion throughout history has developed elaborate beliefs concerning the afterlife.

In its most basic form, necromancy is simply an effort by the living to connect with the dead. Whether this is done through prayer and study or by summoning the dead in a cemetery, the intent is the same. Sorcerers hope to learn about the future from someone who passed from this world a long, long time ago.

CHAPTER 5

Working on the Astral Plane

In his 1929 book *Magick in Theory and Practice*, Aleister Crowley wrote, "Within the human body there is another body of approximately the same size and shape but made of subtler . . . material."[50] Crowley was referring to what is often called the astral body, which he defined as a body of magical light that travels in a mystical dimension known as the astral plane.

Science has never proved the existence of the astral body or the astral plane. However, astral projection, or astral travel, has been central to magical belief for hundreds of years. Sorcerers believe that traveling to the astral plane allows them to see all and do all. As Wiccan author Migene González-Wippler explains: "The astral plane is the working ground of the magician. In that tenuous and dreamlike world he can find the truth about things past and things to come. He can also find the gods, demons, gnomes, fairies . . . archangels, angels, and elemental forces of nature. The astral plane holds both the secret of power and the key to the creation of [magic]."[51]

Everywhere and Continually

Astral travel is sometimes referred to as an out-of-body experience. During this experience, the astral body purportedly leaves the physical body but remains attached to it by an infinitely long silver cord. The astral traveler is conscious and aware that the body has been left behind.

The concept that each person has an astral body that can separate from the physical body is ancient. Thousands of years ago Plato wrote about the astral body, suggesting that humans were composed of three elements. Plato described these elements as the mortal body, immortal reason, and an immortal spirit he called an astral or star soul (*astral* means "star" in Latin). According to Plato, when humans die their astral soul travels throughout the solar system, visiting the moon, sun, and planets. The astral soul is then reincarnated, or brought back to life in the mortal body once again. Plato's concept of a star soul was revived by philosophers and sorcerers during the Renaissance. In the 1500s Heinrich Cornelius Agrippa described the astral body in terms common to the era: "[We] must know, that . . . the soul [has] a certain spiritual light, when it is loosed from the body, it comprehendeth every place and time, in such a manner as a light enclosed in a [lantern], which being open, [diffuses] it self every where, and faileth not any where, for it is every where, and continually."[52]

The Mirror of Imagination

Interest in the spiritual light that shined everywhere and all the time was central to the magic revival of the nineteenth century. Eliphas Levi wrote extensively about the astral light. He echoed

Plato, the classical Greek philosopher and writer, wrote that humans were composed of mortal bodies, immortal reason, and an immortal spirit that he called an astral soul. He believed that the astral soul travels throughout the solar system when a person dies.

Plato when he wrote that humans are composed of three substances, a spiritual soul, a material body, and what he called a plastic medium. (Levi used the term *plastic* in its original sense to mean something easily shaped and molded.)

According to Levi, the existence of the plastic medium was a scientific fact. The medium formed from astral light that the body absorbed from the astral plane. Levi believed a person could control astral light with his or her soul, dissolving, projecting, and otherwise shaping it. According to Levi, the astral light "is the mirror of the imagination and of dreams. It reacts upon the nervous system, and thus produces the movements of the body. The light can [expand] itself indefinitely [to reach] considerable distances. . . . It can take all forms evoked by thought."[53]

Raising the Vibration

While philosophers and magicians wrote about the supernatural aspects of the astral light, the astral force is thought to exist in every person. Because of the universal nature of the astral body, some believe astral travel is not limited to sorcerers. This concept is backed by the Lucidity Institute, which conducts research into dreaming and out-of-body experiences. According to a 2004 institute study, about 20 percent of all people believe they have experienced astral travel at least one time. The experience was often involuntary, caused by an accident, near-death experience, or simply a lucid dream. Some describe astral travel as hellish and horrible, while others compare it to paradise.

Whether the experience is profoundly moving or deeply disturbing, those who engage in astral projection have strikingly similar experiences. Astral travelers feel a surging sense of energy accompanied by odd sounds, such as a humming, hissing, or roaring in the ears. Sometimes, beautiful, unearthly music is heard, a sound described as a large group of instruments backed by a deep roaring sound similar to the crashing waves of the ocean.

Sorcerers believe astral travel allows them to accomplish many tasks. On the astral plane, sorcerers say, they can travel throughout the universe, observe the actions of people thousands of miles away, and spy on rivals. González-Wippler explains:

> One may travel from one region of the astral [plane] to another simply by an act of will that raises the vibration of the astral body without moving it. . . . In other words, if one has the knowledge and

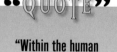

"Within the human body there is another body of approximately the same size and shape."

—Sorcerer Aleister Crowley describing the nature of the astral body.

power one may traverse the entire astral plane, witness its scenery and inhabitants, phenomena and activity, and then return to the material plane, all in a moment of time without [moving].[54]

In the nineteenth century sorcerers of the Golden Dawn began actively experimenting with trances and spells to engage in controlled astral projection. They developed several techniques that are used by believers. To travel to the astral plane, sorcerers lie on the ground and envision their astral body moving around the room. According to ceremonial magician Francis King, the experience involves mentally inhabiting the astral body and taking control: "Formulate [the astral body] in your mind's eye standing in robes and holding a dagger. Project your consciousness into this form, open its eyes, and try to see through them. In the [astral] form go to the East. Make yourself 'feel' there by looking around, touching the wall, shifting the feet and so on."[55] Once this state has been achieved, the sorcerer can purportedly project the astral body into an adjoining room, walk through walls, and visit a friend who lives far away.

"The Mighty Mother Isis"

Astral travelers believe they can shape their experiences by using tarot cards as magical charms to enhance supernatural experiences. The cards of the tarot deck contain symbols that represent power, fertility, prosperity, romance, travel, justice, death, and eternal life. Sorcerers believe that when they focus on a specific tarot card during astral projection, they can enter the universe symbolized by the card. In one example provided by King, an unnamed woman used the Empress, said to be one of the most powerful tarot cards, for this purpose. The Empress symbolizes beauty, love, happiness, pleasure, good fortune, and marriage.

According to King, the Empress was placed before the woman, who stared at it intently. She claimed her astral body was projected onto the astral plane into a world inhabited by the Empress. In a place of heavenly beauty, the woman said she felt herself rising through the clouds until she stood before a towering temple made of ghostly lines and points of light. She purportedly walked past a friendly green dragon and stepped onto a radiantly white marble terrace that overlooked a fantastic green garden. Suddenly, a goddess appeared, wearing a green gown, a jeweled vest, and a crown of stars. She held a gold scepter in one hand and a glass orb etched with a cross in the other. When the astral traveler asked the goddess for her name, according to King, she replied:

> I am the mighty Mother Isis; most powerful of all the world. I am she who fights not, but is always victorious, I am that Sleeping Beauty who men have sought, for all time: and the paths which lead to my castle are beset with dangers and illusions. [Those who] fail to find me sleep. . . . I am the worlds' desire, but few find me. When my secret is told, it is the secret of the Holy Grail. . . . This is love, I have plucked out my heart and have given it to the world; that is my strength. Love is the Mother of Man—God, giving . . . her life to save mankind from destruction, and to show forth the path of life eternal.[56]

After the experience, the astral traveler returned to her physical body. She experienced extremely powerful feelings of courage and stopped fearing death. As a witness to the experience, King writes, "Our own hearts were to be henceforth in touch with [Isis]—the strongest force in all the world."[57]

Sorcerers claim they can enter the universe symbolized in a tarot card by focusing on that card during astral projection. According to one account, the powerful Empress card (top right) provided just such a passage.

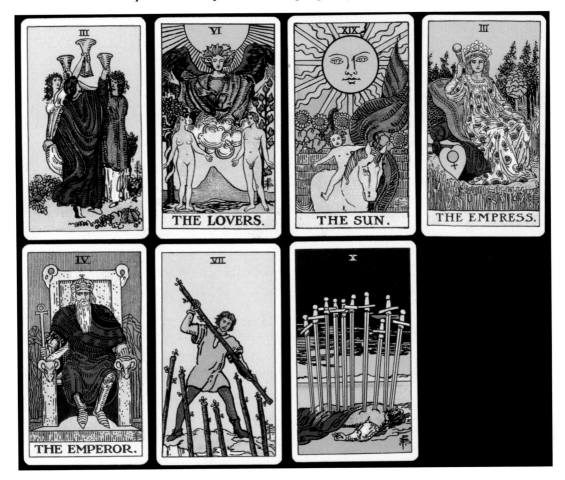

The Astral Attack

Crowley was a strong believer in the astral body and said it was central to executing all magical desires. He wrote that skillful sorcerers should be able to glide in and out of the astral light as easily as slipping in and out of a dressing gown. However, Crowley also thought that if this state were not achieved through proper ritual, the sorcerer could be in serious trouble. The astral body might wander away uncontrolled or provoke attacks by wayward spirits. This might result in physical and emotional problems, including headaches, nightmares, hysteria, fainting, paralysis, or madness.

Crowley claimed to have used astral travel for both cosmic and mundane matters. He explained that traveling to the astral light was helpful in a case where a pickpocket had stolen his watch. Although he did not know who the thief was, or where he was, Crowley allegedly established a link to his missing watch on the astral plane and attracted helpful spirits in the astral dimension. The spirits supposedly acted as cosmic police, hunting down the thief, terrifying him mentally, and compelling him to return the watch at once. Crowley stopped short of saying whether he recovered his watch.

Crowley was more sinister when writing about his quest to win the love of a woman who actively disliked him and loved another man. Crowley claimed to have sent his astral body to enter and take control of the woman's mind. Crowley explains:

> I may work "naturally" by wooing, of course. But, magically, I may attack her astrally so that her [astral body] becomes uneasy, responding no longer to her lover. Unless they diagnose the cause, a quarrel may result, and the woman's bewildered and hun-

gry Body of Light may turn in its distress to that of the Magician [Crowley] who has mastered it.[58]

Crowley acknowledges that many things can go wrong in this scenario. The lover might possess more powerful magic than Crowley, or the woman may be astrally mismatched to the sorcerer. Crowley might even have deceived himself into thinking he loved the woman when he actually did not. No amount of astral sorcery could overcome this delusion. As Crowley writes, "There is opportunity for all kinds of error in the transmission of the [astral light]; misunderstanding may mar the matter; a mood may make mischief; external events may interfere . . . the Operation may offend nature in many ways."[59] Whatever the risks or rewards, Crowley stated that it should be the aim of every sorcerer to obtain comprehensive knowledge of the astral light.

Shape-Shifters

Sorcerers believe the astral body has other uses. One involves its transformation into an animal in a process is called shape-shifting. Over the centuries, the astral bodies of sorcerers have been said to appear as coyotes, wolves, foxes, nighthawks, bats, and even cats and dogs. In 1923 a student of Crowley's named W.B. Seabrook provided an example of a Russian woman named Nastatia Filipovna shifting into an animal during astral travel. This transformation was prompted by the magical symbolism of a divinatory book called the *I Ching*.

The *I Ching* has been used to predict the future in China for nearly 4,000 years. The book is based on 64 simple, 6-line columns called hexagrams. Each hexagram has a written description that symbolizes a human trait or situation in life. When Seabrook used the book, he meditated on specific hexagrams in the *I Ching*

Unsuccessful astral travel might result in physical and emotion problems that include headaches, nightmares, hysteria, fainting, paralysis, or madness.

Crowley's Astral Light

Aleister Crowley was a strong believer in the astral body, which he called the astral light. He wrote that all sorcery should be conducted on the astral plane. In his 1911 book, *Magick in Theory and Practice*, Crowley described and defined the astral light:

> In that Light, objects can change their appearance completely without suffering change of Nature. The same [object] can reveal itself in an infinite number of different aspects. . . . In that Light one is swift without feet and flying without wings; one can travel without moving, and communicate without conventional means of expression. One is insensible to heat, cold, pain, and other forms of apprehension. . . . In the Astral Light we are bound by what is, superficially, an entirely different series of laws. We meet with obstacles of a strange and subtle character; and we overcome them by an energy and cunning of an order entirely alien to that which serves us in an earthly life. In the light, symbols are not conventions but realities of our own nature.

Aleister Crowley, *Magick in Theory and Practice*. New York: Castle, 1960, p. 83.

to inspire astral travel. In doing so, he purportedly transformed into a monk in eleventh-century Italy.

Yelps and Slaverings

When Filipovna used the *I Ching* to aid astral travel, she picked the hexagram called Ko. In its original meaning, Ko represents an animal's pelt, which changes over the course of the year by molting. In its magical symbolism, this molting represents great revolutions.

During the astral projection process, Seabrook worked with an assistant named Bannister. To initiate the astral process, Filipovna knelt in a dark room and stared at a door. Nothing happened for three hours except for Filipovna complaining of aching knees. Eventually, she began an astral journey driven by the image of Ko, the animal pelt. Seabrook wrote down her words, uttered haltingly as she entered the astral plane:

> The door is moving. The door is opening. But it's opening into the outdoors. . . . Snow . . . everywhere snow . . . the moon is white snow . . . and black trees there against the sky. I am lying in the snow . . . wearing a fur coat . . . I am warm in the snow. . . . It is good to lie warm in the snow . . . I am moving now . . . I am crawling on my hands and knees . . . I'm not crawling now, I'm running on my hands and feet, lightly . . . I'm running like the wind . . . how good the snow smells. . . . And there's another good smell. Ah! Ah! Faster. . . . Faster![60]

By this time Filipovna was panting and breathing rapidly. According to Seabrook, he became alarmed when Filipovna began making "sounds that were not human. There were yelps, slaverings,

"QUOTE"

"There were yelps, slaverings, panting and then a deep baying such as only two sorts of animals on earth emit when they are running—wolves and hounds."

—Sorcerer W.B. Seabrook describing the noises emitted by Nastatia Filipovna during astral travel.

panting and then a deep baying such as only two sorts of animals on earth emit when they are running—wolves and hounds."[61] In order to bring her out of the astral experience, Bannister slapped Filipovna's face several times. Instead of waking up, she lunged at Bannister and attempted to rip his throat open with her teeth. He fought her off successfully, and she retreated to a corner of the room, where she cowered and shook. Seabrook and Bannister threw blankets over Filipovna to contain her movements and, after a struggle, placed a bottle of ammonia smelling salts under her nose. She soon regained consciousness. She was given a glass of brandy but said little.

Astral Vampires

When Filipovna's astral body shifted into a canine, she assumed the shape accidentally. However, some sorcerers ostensibly turn themselves into horrifying creatures on purpose to wreak havoc with black magic. One of these monsters is called the cannibalistic astral vampire. Sorcerers who obtain this form gain power by feeding on the souls of enemies.

When an astral vampire attacks a person, the creature flies into a house, lifts the prey from the bed, and throws him or her to the floor. The victim writhes in agony as the vampire slowly consumes the astral body. The pain feels as if some invisible force is drinking the blood and eating the entrails and heart. The attack leaves the target sickened, weak, and desiccated. But the process extends the life of the astral vampire. Michael W. Ford, founder of the Luciferian Magical Order, comments on astral vampires (sometimes spelled "vampyres"): "The symbol of the vampyre who drinks blood from sleeping humans is not far removed from the astral vampyre predator who drains the lifeforce from the sleeping human's astral body."[62]

Stories of astral vampires who drain the life force from the astral bodies of sleeping humans originated in Transylvania (pictured), a region usually associated with the bloodsucking vampires of folk tales and fiction.

Tales of the astral vampire originated in Transylvania, a region of northern Romania often associated with bloodsucking vampires like the fictional Count Dracula. The Transylvanians call the astral vampire vârcolac or varcolaci (plural). It appears as a wolf demon with many hungry mouths or as a hellish winged dragon.

The astral body of the vârcolac rises from its physical form at midnight to feed. The creature searches for an old woman who is spinning thread alone in her home, and it attaches its silver astral cord to the wool thread. This causes the victim to bleed from her ears, eyes, nose, and mouth. She continues to spin, and her thread becomes an astral cord that reaches the moon. According to Ford, this cord is a bridge for the vârcolac that allows it to "wander the dark portals of the cosmos to attack the heavenly bodies. . . . During this [time] the vampyre is able to shape shift at will. The Varcolaci will rise especially when the moon turns a blood red or copper color. The dark spirits will then drink astral blood from the moon, stars, or the sleeping."[63]

Many sorcerers oppose astral vampirism because of the harm it brings to both the victim's soul and physical body. This negative energy is also likely to bring ruin upon those who attempt to imitate the varcolaci. As Levi writes, astral vampires are "like children playing with fire in the neighborhood of a cask of gunpowder, sooner or later they will fall victims to some terrible explosion."[64]

The Belief in Sorcery Lives On

Like all forms of sorcery, astral travel has long been controversial because it seems to interfere with the natural order. Some believe life is a set of random occurrences guided by scientific principles. Others think that only God can guide human enterprise. Sorcerers contradict these views. They imagine the physical world can be controlled through ceremonies, spells, magical potions, and astral travel. Little wonder then that sorcery has been condemned, ridiculed, and outlawed for centuries. Whatever the controversies, sorcery is based on concepts that are over 2,000 years old. With roots in ancient Greece and Egypt, the magical methods have remained remarkably consistent for millennia. And the spirits of deceased sorcerers like Aleister Crowley, John Dee, and Eliphas Levi continue to influence sorcerers and others who believe in magic in the modern digital world.

NOTES

Introduction: Making Magic

1. Quoted in Montague Summers, *The History of Witchcraft and Demonology*. New York: Citadel, 1993, p. 1.
2. P.G. Maxwell-Stuart, *Wizards: A History*. Gloucestershire: Tempus, 2004, p. 11.
3. Maxwell-Stuart, *Wizards*, p. 10.

Chapter 1: Sorcery Through the Ages

4. Benvenuto Cellini, *The Autobiography of Benvenuto Cellini*. Echo Library: Teddington, UK, 2007, p. 98.
5. *Papyri Graecae Magicae*, Hermitic Library, 2011. http://hermetic.com/pgm.
6. *Papyri Graecae Magicae*.
7. *Papyri Graecae Magicae*.
8. Plato, *The Republic*, Internet Classics Archive, 2009. http://classics.mit.edu.
9. Quoted in Centre for the Study of Ancient Documents, "Curse Tablets from Roman Britain: Uly 72," October 27, 2009. www.csad.ox.ac.uk.
10. Quoted in Centre for the Study of Ancient Documents, "Curse Tablets from Roman Britain."
11. L.S. Davidson and J.O. Ward, *The Sorcery Trial of Alice Kyteler*. Binghamton, NY: Medival and Renaissance Texts & Studies, 1993, p. 5.
12. Quoted in Davidson and Ward, *The Sorcery Trial of Alice Kyteler*, p. 29.
13. Quoted in Davidson and Ward, *The Sorcery Trial of Alice Kyteler*, p. 28.
14. Quoted in Davidson and Ward, *The Sorcery Trial of Alice Kyteler*, p. 28.

Chapter 2: Sorcerers and Ceremonies

15. Eliphas Levi and A.E. Waite, *Dogme et Rituel de la Haute Magie, Part I: The Doctrine of Transcendental Magic*. London: Rider, 1896, p. 1.
16. Eliphas Levi and A.E. Waite, *Dogme et Rituel de la Haute Magie, Part II: The Ritual of Transcendental Magic*. London: Rider, 1896, p. 10.
17. Levi and Waite, *Dogme et Rituel de la Haute Magie, Pt. II*, p. 73.
18. Levi and Waite, *Dogme et Rituel de la Haute Magie, Pt. II*, p. 74.
19. Levi and Waite, *Dogme et Rituel de la Haute Magie, Pt. II*, p. 74.
20. Levi and Waite, *Dogme et Rituel de la Haute Magie, Pt. II*, p. 75.
21. Frederick Hockley, *The Rosicrucian Seer: The Magical Writings of Frederick Hockley*, ed. John Hamill. Wellingborough, UK: Aquarian, 1986, pp. 130–31.
22. Israel Regardie, *The Golden Dawn*. St. Paul: Llewellyn, 1984, p. 17.
23. Maxwell-Stuart, *Wizards*, p. 177.
24. Maxwell-Stuart, *Wizards*, p. 193.
25. Aleister Crowley, *The Book of the Law*, Sacred Texts, 2010. www.sacred-texts.com.
26. Quoted in Kenneth Grant, *Magical Revival*. New York: Weiser, 1973, p. 5.

Chapter 3: Charms, Potions, and Powders

27. Paul Beyerl, *The Master Book of Herbalism*. Custer, WA: Phoenix, 1984, p. 262.

28. Scott Cunningham, *Crystal, Gem & Metal Magic*. St. Paul: Llewellyn, 1991, p. 99.
29. Ray T. Malbrough, *Charms, Spells & Formulas*. St. Paul: Llewellyn, 1986, p. 15.
30. Malbrough, *Charms, Spells & Formulas*, p. 49.
31. Paul Huson, *Wicca: Mastering Witchcraft*. New York: Putnam's Sons, 1970, p. 20.
32. William Shakespeare, *Macbeth*, Complete Works of William Shakespeare, 2011. http://shakespeare.mit.edu.
33. Levi and Waite, *Dogme et Rituel de la Haute Magie, Pt. I*, p. 89.
34. Levi and Waite, *Dogme et Rituel de la Haute Magie, Pt. I*, pp. 89–90.
35. Quoted in Archibald Cockren, "Alchemy Rediscovered and Restored," Sacred Texts, 2011. www.sacred-texts.com.

Chapter 4: Summoning the Dead

36. Daniel Ogden, *Greek and Roman Necromancy*. Princeton, NJ: Princeton University Press, 2001, p. xvii.
37. Levi and Waite, *Dogme et Rituel de la Haute Magie, Pt. I*, p. 64.
38. Levi and Waite, *Dogme et Rituel de la Haute Magie, Pt. II*, p. 74.
39. Heinrich Cornelius Agrippa, "Heinrich Cornelius Agrippa: Of Occult Philosophy, Book III (part 4)," Esoteric Archives, 2000. www.esotericarchives.com.
40. Quoted in Maxwell-Stuart, *Wizards*, p. 92.
41. John Dee and Edward Kelley, "The Forty-Eight Calls," Hermetic Library, 2011. http://hermetic.com.
42. John Dee, *Mysteriorum Liber Primus*, John Dee Publication Project, 1999. www.john-dee.org.
43. Quoted in Maxwell-Stuart, *Wizards*, p. 93.
44. Huson, *Wicca*, p. 66.
45. Quoted in Donald Joralemon and Douglas Sharon, *Sorcery and Shamanism*. Salt Lake City: University of Utah Press, 1993, p. 105.
46. Quoted in Joralemon and Sharon, *Sorcery and Shamanism*, p. 108.
47. Huson, *Wicca*, p. 85.
48. Huson, *Wicca*, p. 86.
49. Quoted in Jon Winokur, "Curmudgeon," *Funny Times*, September 2011, p. 22.

Chapter 5: Working on the Astral Plane

50. Aleister Crowley, *Magick in Theory and Practice*. New York: Castle, 1960, p. 101.
51. Migene González-Wippler, *The Complete Book of Spells, Ceremonies & Magic*. St. Paul: Llewellyn, 1988, p. 98.
52. Agrippa, "Heinrich Cornelius Agrippa."
53. Eliphas Levi, *The Key of the Mysteries*. New York: Red Wheel, 2002, p. 52.
54. González-Wippler, *The Complete Book of Spells, Ceremonies & Magic*, p. 103.
55. Francis King, *Techniques of High Magic*. Rochester, VT: Destiny, 1976, p. 101.
56. Quoted in Francis King, *Astral Projection, Ritual Magic, and Alchemy*. Rochester, VT: Destiny, 1987, pp. 72–73.
57. King, *Astral Projection, Ritual Magic, and Alchemy*, p. 73.
58. Crowley, *Magick in Theory and Practice*, p. 87.
59. Crowley, *Magick in Theory and Practice*, p. 87.
60. Quoted in King, *Techniques of High Magic*, p. 96.
61. Quoted in King, *Techniques of High Magic*, p. 96.
62. Michael W. Ford, *Book of Wamphyri and Shadows*, Dark Books, 2011. http://darkbooks.org.
63. Ford, *Book of Wamphyri and Shadows*.
64. Levi and Waite, *Dogme et Rituel de la Haute Magie, Pt. I*, p. 33.

Books

Rosemary Ellen Guiley, *Witches and Wiccans*. New York: Checkmark, 2009.

Stuart A. Kallen, *Communication with the Dead*. San Diego: ReferencePoint, 2009.

Jason Karl, *The Secret World of Witchcraft*. Middlesex, UK: New Holland, 2009.

Allan Zola Kronzek and Elizabeth Kronzek, *The Sorcerer's Companion: A Guide to the Magical World of Harry Potter*. New York: Broadway, 2010.

Gienna Matson, *Celtic Mythology A to Z*. New York: Chelsea House, 2010.

Robert Michael Place, *Magic and Alchemy*. New York: Chelsea House, 2009.

Websites

Aleister Crowley, Controverscial.com (www.controverscial.com/Aleister%20 Crowley.htm). A biography of the most controversial sorcerer of the twentieth century, with links to biographies of many Crowley colleagues, including Arthur E. Waite and MacGregor Mathers. The comprehensive site also features dozens of articles covering Wicca and witchcraft, magical stones and gems, and other sorcery-related subjects.

Crystalinks (www.crystalinks.com). This site contains over 10,000 articles on the occult, supernatural, and magic, with detailed essays on astral projection, alchemy, divination, sorcery, necromancy, and other metaphysical subjects.

Grimoires, Internet Sacred Text Archive (www.sacred-texts.com/grim/index .htm). This massive archive holds electronic texts about religion, mythology, legends and folklore, and the occult. The "Grimoire" page features texts from the nineteenth and twentieth centuries written by modern sorcerers such as Aleister Crowley, Arthur E. Waite, and Francis Barrett.

Hermetic Library (http://hermetic.com). Created in 1996, this site is one of the most comprehensive resources on the Internet, with texts about magic and sorcery from ancient times through the twentieth century.

Sorcery, *The Skeptic's Dictionary* (www .skepdic.com/sorcery.html). Site author Robert T. Carroll has written a wide array of articles on this site that debunk widespread beliefs in paranormal and supernatural phenomena. The "Sorcery" page has links to articles that shine a skeptical light on black magic, divination, spells, and Satan.

INDEX

Note: Boldface page numbers indicate illustrations.

Picture Credits

Cover: Thinkstock/Hemera

The Archangel Michael (tempera on panel), Guariento, Ridolfo di Arpo (c.1310-c.1370) / Museo Civico, Padua, Italy / The Bridgeman Art Library International: 70

© Historical Picture Archive/Corbis: 79

© Blue Lantern Studio/Corbis: 9, 55

© Julie Dermansky/Corbis: 49

The Last Judgement, detail of Satan devouring the damned in hell, c.1431 (oil on panel), Angelico, Fra (Guido di Pietro) (c.1387-1455) / Museo di San Marco dell'Angelico, Florence, Italy / Giraudon / The Bridgeman Art Library International: 31

© Floris Leeuwenberg/The Cover Story/Corbis: 37

© Edwardo Munoz/Reuters/Corbis: 60

Michael Nicholson/Corbis: 15

Photofest: 40

© Leonard de Selva/Corbis: 22

Thinkstock/Hermera: 85

Thinkstock/Photos.com: 75

The Weird Sisters, Macbeth, Act IV Scene 1, illustration from 'Tales from Shakespeare' by Charles and Mary Lamb, 1905 (colour litho), Price, Norman Mills (1877-1951) (after) / Private Collection / The Stapleton Collection / The Bridgeman Art Library International: 52

ABOUT THE AUTHOR

Stuart A. Kallen is the author of more than 250 nonfiction books for children and young adults. He has written on topics ranging from the theory of relativity to the history of rock and roll. In addition, Kallen has written award-winning children's videos and television scripts. In his spare time he is a singer/songwriter/guitarist in San Diego.